LOVE:
FROM
THE DARKNESS
INTO THE LIGHT

By
J. Wayne Frye

LOVE: FROM THE DARKNESS TO THE LIGHT

The Author

Wayne Frye's Aaron Adams series, Girl books and Lynton adventures have been popular among Canadian mystery lovers since first appearing in 2005. He provides satirical political commentary to many Canadian newspapers, and his books on politics have created a great deal of controversy. He has written marketing/ advertising textbooks, been a successful U.S. university hockey coach, professor, university president and served as a marketing consultant to hockey teams and motion picture companies. He has been cited for his work with inner-city gang children in the Los Angeles area and been active in the anti-globalization movement. He became a Canadian citizen in 2003 and divides his time between Ladysmith, Vancouver Island, British Columbia and Cavite, Philippines.

Other Books by J. Wayne Frye

Hockey Mania and the Mystery of Nancy Running Elk
Something Evil in the Darkness at Hopkins House
How Hockey Saved a Jew From the Holocaust:
The Rudi Ball Story
The Catastrophic Calamities of a Village Idiot
Fighting for Justice in the Land of Hypocrisy
Guide to Alternative Education (13 Editions)
Cataclysmic Dreams in Black and White
Introduction to Advertising
Lynton Curls Her Hair
Lynton Buys a New Cell Phone and Hears the Voice of Doom
Lynton Walks On Water While Ingrid & Channa do an Irish Jig
Lynton and the Vampire at Tagaytay Manor
Fall From Apocalypse
Armageddon Now
Worth
When Jesus Came to Jersey as the Son of Thunder
The Girl Who Danced with the Demons of Darkness
The Girl Who Stirred Up the Whirlwind
The Girl Who Motivated Murder Most Foul
The Girl Who Said Goodbye for the Last Time
The Girl Who Made Love to the Yeti in Kathmandu
Canadian Angels of Mercy – Nurses in Times of Peril
Points of Rebellion: Aboriginals Who Fought for Justice
Chablis: Avenging Angel for the Forgotten
In the City of Lost Hope
Chablis and the Terrorist Who Resurrected the Spirit of Che Guevara
Musings from the Edge

LOVE: FROM THE DARKNESS TO THE LIGHT

TABLE OF CONTENTS

PROLOGUE

Promise and Optimism

Page 5

PART 1

**Loss of Hope at a Moment in Time
That Was to be Transitory**

Page 7

PART 2
**In Pursuit of an Ideal that Proclaims
Love Can be Lost and Love Can be Found**

Page 70

PART 3

**The Frivolity of That Which Was
Fostered From the Motivation
Provided By My Muse**

Page 155

LOVE: FROM THE DARKNESS TO THE LIGHT

TO:

*My muse and my life, Lynton Globa Viñas,
The woman who led me into the light.*

Copyright 2014 by J. Wayne Frye
All rights reserved. No part of this book or covers may be reproduced or transmitted in any form or by any other means, electronic or mechanical, including photocopying, recording, or by any information storage and retrieval system, without permission from the author.

ISBN: 978-1-928183-07-5

Fireside Books – Victoria, British Columbia
Peninsula Publishing Consortium

LOVE: FROM THE DARKNESS TO THE LIGHT

PROLOGUE
PROMISE AND OPTIMISM

My dear muse, Lynton Viñas, urged me to put some of my love-related poetry into a semblance of order and share it with the handful of loyal fans I have who read my Aaron Adams, Chablis Louise Chavez and Lynton mysteries. Well, here it is at her behest. I have tried to concentrate on the last few years of my life and how it was often filled with turmoil, so that those who suffer as I did can know that someone else has shared their pain. Although I served in the military during wartime, I am probably one of the most non-violent persons alive, because I see violence as a prescription for disaster. You can observe the Bush wars in Afghanistan and Iraq as prime examples of how resorting to violence only leads to more violence. Think about what a different world we would have today, if Bush had not had to prove his manhood to himself and daddy by sending thousands of Americans out to die in senseless, useless, illegal wars. A heavy price is paid for stupidity. Unfortunately, often those who initiate the stupidity are not always the ones who pay the price. .

Looking back on my own stupidity, I know that life is a circuitous road, not a thoroughfare. The roads are not straight but curved. They are not level but are filled with hills and potholes. So, as will be observed in my prose, I went through a period of deep darkness and despair, but for those of my readers who might now be experiencing that misery in their own lives, I say that all is not lost, and that hopelessness is generally a transitory condition.

You will note that my prose starts out with great moroseness, only to be followed by a period of tranquility. I have found that what is one day's tragedy can lead to another day's euphoria, because without that tragedy, the

LOVE: FROM THE DARKNESS TO THE LIGHT

door to a better life might not have been opened. So, when one door closes another usually opens.

I am in the later stages of my life now, but I am facing eternity with the realization that my life has not been wasted. I have suffered pain and heartache often, but that misery has led to a realization that I have many people who love and value me. I never realized until the tragedy that befell me in 2013 that I had so many people who loved and appreciated me. Through my turmoil, my dear children returned the compassion and love I had always showed them, making me realize that I was not a failure as a father. My relatives and friends reached out to me with concern and kindness that made me understand that though we had been separated by time and distance, they still had love for me. Even people whom I did not realize were my friends came forward to embrace me in my time of need. So, through the pain, agony and tears I saw the bright sunshine of love. I once told myself, as I was in the depths of my despair, that I was incredibly unlucky, but how unlucky can a man be who has people say "Wayne you made a difference in my life," or "Wayne you never wavered in your commitment to fight injustice," or simply, "Wayne, I love you."

As I wrote many of these poems and verses, I scribed them through tears, but those tears are me. They are the drops of passion from my heart – a heart that is still beating, though humbled and scarred from pain. Right now, I see a bright sun rising to cast its warmth on a day of hope. It may eventually be covered with dark clouds harbouring storms of discontent, and it will definitely go down and bring darkness as it always does, but I know I have a bright candle of anticipation and optimism glowing in the darkness to light my way to promise and optimism.

LOVE: FROM THE DARKNESS TO THE LIGHT

PART 1: LOSS OF HOPE AT A MOMENT IN TIME THAT WAS TO BE TRANSITORY

In 2013, my wife of 20 years left me to run into the arms of another man. Now, I know that I am not unique when it comes to circumstances like this, but each one of us experiencing that kind of pain does indeed think that we are alone in having to face the agony of love lost.

I went though an incredibly morose period as a result of my wife deciding to be with this other man for reasons that are not really germane to this particular book, and Part 1 deals with that period when I was, I thought, helplessly lost in a sea of misery where there was no safe harbour in sight.

TO HIS HEART SHE HOLDS THE KEY

Her champion would not bend in the wind
No matter how much he was chagrined.
Hope springs eternal in his emptiness,
That she will help him escape the darkness.

To himself he is less than the cloud to the wind,
To himself he is less than the foam to the sea,
To himself he is less than the rose to the storm
He only wants the good in himself for her to see.

To him she is brighter than the stars at night,
She is more than the rain to the lea,
She is more than heaven to the earth
To his stilled heart, she holds the key.

THE TRUTH BE KNOWN

I come back to let you know
that I am dead inside.

LOVE: FROM THE DARKNESS TO THE LIGHT

I am not at peace.
I long for your love.
Mine was a senseless death in your heart.
How senseless and cruel.
But when I realized the truth,
It was too late ... too late.
I shall not rest
Until the truth be known.

THAT WHICH ABIDES IN THE WIND

Do not whisper to the wind,
For a spectre is waiting there.
With anxious sighs and open ears,
Just listening to the sullen air.
Waiting for someone who cares,
To answer and become aware.

Do not whisper to the wind,
For a spectre comes leather skinned,
With eyes aglow in sickly hue,
A floating figure tall and thinned.
You may not, shall not, can not
Ever whisper to the wind!

ONLY LOVE WILL FREE ME

Close your eyes, darkness is deep.
My lover is in peaceful sleep with another.
Inside her heart, no remorse,
But she did not reckon a ghostly force.

Mirrors of lies chant my name,
As she plays a heartless game.
Nightmares will flow through her mind
because ghostly spectres of the past build my shrine.

LOVE: FROM THE DARKNESS TO THE LIGHT

Her new love imprisons her.
She needs the truth that only I can see.
Despair was my earthly fate.
Only her love will free me, so I wait.

THE MAN WITH THE SCYTHE

As the rain pounded the pavement at my feet
And the wind bit bitterly through my coat,
I realized the rain was like the tears
I have shed now for too many years.

I loved a woman so much, but did not know,
That some of my actions would make her go.
An ill wind swept into my home one night,
And a Svengali did a magic spell skilfully weave,
Stealing she who was my breath of life,
Sowing deep seeds of heartless strife.

Though time is supposed to heal all wounds,
In my mind I can still hear sweet loons,
Uttering the refrain that bounces about my brain
Slowly, methodically driving me insane.
When will the pain finally end within my heart,
And from this misery I can cheerfully depart?

From Apocalypse down rides the horseman,
Swinging his deathly scythe all about,
And how I want to bow and shout,
"Take me, take me, please sweep me away,
And in the belly of eternity I can quietly lay."
Only then will I finally be OK.

TRUTH'S SANCTITY

The grimness of the grave

LOVE: FROM THE DARKNESS TO THE LIGHT

cannot hold the truth in abeyance.
The truth will from its trap escape.
It will look upon the sullen world
to see only lies and deceit.
But alas, she will seek the truth.
She is a breath, a wind,
a shadow, a phantom.
Long shall she pursue truth,
undeterred by the mountain of lies
her new lover lays before her.
In the sweet bye and bye,
She will realize what she lost.
She shall know truth's sanctity.

IT EMBRACES ME NOW

I am told the pain
will ease with time.
That I will think
of her without a tear.
But that is impossible,
because I need her here.
Our love was interrupted
by something evil and foul.
Oh, the cold ground,
it embraces me now.

LOVE LOST IN RECRIMNATIONS

How strangely blind is love.
It can be humanity's greatest foe!
She who once loved me
never fails to see wrong
but naught of good can know.
'Tis blind to all that's lofty, to truth it is opposed.
Degrading things will open eyes,

LOVE: FROM THE DARKNESS TO THE LIGHT

but the good keep them closed.
How cruel is love! How wicked is the tongue!
The evils reign supremely there in her heart.
The bad is ever sung.
It is my greatest curse.
It festers like an open sore.
It slowly saps precious life.
It is poison to the core.

WITHOUT LOVE

A statue can stand with a head of gold,
Seeming to emit pride brash and bold.
And its breast with polished silver may shine.
Ah, and it can have brass on its lower spine.
Iron can make the legs seem strong.
But without a core things go wrong.
Beneath, it may be built of miry clay
And reinforced with iron to prevent sway.
But Without truth it can not and will not stand.
Without love it crumbles to the ground.

DISMISSIVE LOVE

Scars from the past,
scars from the present,
scars from every hidden teardrop
that precipitously falls,
hiding the truth from all.
Concealing the cuts deep within the heart,
No one knows the truth of the love I have for her.
No one but me, and she
who now dismisses it without a care.

QUOTE: Love is an ember that can sparkle and blaze anew or it can slowly fade away and disappear into ash.

LOVE: FROM THE DARKNESS TO THE LIGHT

THE TRUTH OF MY LOVE

When truth comes, the landscape listens.
Shadows hold their breath in anticipation.
When truth lights the night with brightness,
Injustice is rectified and sanctity prevails.
Oh please heaven let her see the truth of my love.

IF SHE LOVES ME AGAIN

Life was a desperate and frantic struggle.
Cursed by the one I loved, I endured unto death.
I was placed in the valley of eternal sleep.
Injustice was the epitaph carved onto my tombstone.
I rose from the darkness of the grave, seeking solace.
If only I could get her to embrace my cold body.
How I ask can I fight her indifference.
The deceit was brought from the shadows into the light.
I can only rest in peace if she loves me again.

A FINAL PLEA

Kindness is a language the blind can see
and the deaf can hear.
Even the dead can sense its power.
Can she whom I love muster it for me?

HER PLEASURE IN DISHING OUT PAIN IS MY BREATH OF LIFE

I long to feel pain inflicted by she whom I defiled.
The sadistic kisses of her verbal assaults are deserved.
The biting pain of her whip is payment for my slights.
Making me crawl and beg brings her delight.
She teases me with wantonness, making me shake.
So, it brings great joy to serve her.

LOVE: FROM THE DARKNESS TO THE LIGHT

With desire to touch her where all men long to touch.
She taunts me with her alluring ways.
I am dancing with pain, but need it for penance.
Making me beg for the slightest pleasure,
She delights as I make myself supine to her desires.
Use me, abuse me, defile me, make me her slave
And I shall welcome it with delight,
For I am not worthy enough to even kiss her feet.
If I lay in her lap dying, a smile will crease my lips
Knowing that my last breath was in service to she,
Who disdainfully discarded me like an old worn out shoe.
I am nothing, and she makes sure I know it.
Thank you. Thank you. Thank you.
I played a dangerous game that
Has now damaged me and cast me
Into the lair of she who shall make me
Pay recompenses the rest of my life.
I embrace the pain of she who taunts me,
Because I know it is well-deserved.
Bowing to her is all I live for.
Her pleasure in dishing out pain is my breath of life.

I AM ALL ALONE WHILE MY WIFE IS GETTING THE BONE

Happy those early days, when I
Shined with the glow from my angel,
Before I understood this place called loneliness,
And now she is with he who gives her boniness.

While I lament at every turn and try to curry favour,
All I do is deemed an affront to decency.
I cry for compassion, reaching out with a plea.
Yet, my deep sorrow and recompense she refuses to see.

She is in his arms now as I sit in pain.

LOVE: FROM THE DARKNESS TO THE LIGHT

Living blissfully in what she thinks is Shangri-La.
Ah heaven, I can understand as I sit all alone.
What she really craves is his stiff bone.

HER COMING FEAR

From the other world, she came lovingly to me.
Her locks uncurled with drenching dew.
I knew the old, while she knew the new.
But tomorrow, she shall know this, too.
The unfurling of my flag of despair
Turns against all that is just and fair.
But from the ashes of my
Sorrow on this distant shore,
A great awakening will be born.
And her presence is but a mist
In a world that I think cannot exist.
Let her see the light that shines in my heart,
And maybe she will no longer stay apart.
She loves someone else but I am always here,
To quietly harmonize and defeat her coming fear.

LIFE IS A MARATHON NOT A 100 METRE DASH

I read of a man who stood to speak
At a funeral of a friend.
He referred to the dates of her life as carved into stone,
From the beginning to the end.

He noted that first came the date of her birth.
As he spoke, down his cheeks were cascading tears,
And then he said what mattered most
Was the date when she left a man she loved for years.

For the time with him was the time she grew as a woman.
It was the golden years of her time on earth.

LOVE: FROM THE DARKNESS TO THE LIGHT

It was a time of both laughter and sadness,
But reviewed in perspective, oh, how much it was worth!

She was left wealthy, but was really poor.
The cars, the house, the cash,
Were small compared to what she lost.
For life is not a 100 metre dash.

You see, life is not a sprint but a marathon.
She sought out another, so desperate was she for change.
But over time she found that what she left
Could have all been accommodatingly rearranged.

If she had slowed down enough and really thought,
And considered what is true and real,
And tried to understand the heart of the man,
She would have known how abiding love makes you feel.

She saw his mind was wracked in turmoil.
Yet, his love and devotion were engrained to his very core.
After he was nothing but dust in the ground, she
Realized expediency had taken what could have been more.

He should have been a better man,
But over his rhythmic cadence was a festering sore.
If only she could have seen the possibilities
That he was capable of so much more.

I read her eulogy long after he who loved her was gone.
If only she had reached for hope rather than to rehash
That which could been tossed into the dustbin of the past,
She would have realized life is a marathon
not a 100 metre dash.

> Love often sets like the sun at evening time.

LOVE: FROM THE DARKNESS TO THE LIGHT

WHEN LOVE FADES

My love for you is like driving a car,
and I am the worst driver in the world.
I missed all the signs and ended up lost.

That is why I wish you could look at me
and see the person you once loved
instead of the person you have grown to hate.

QUIET DESPERATION

I once looked in the mirror each morning
and saw a tight, taunt, youthful, exuberant face.
Today, I look forlornly in the mirror and see
a bewildered, wrinkled, saggy chinned old man.
People can not see through my façade of gregariousness.
They, no doubt, say "that man has got it together."
But the truth is I lead a life of quiet desperation,
and on a slender thread do I precariously tether.

THE OTHER HALF OF MY HEART

I never knew I could feel so much pain,
and yet be so in love with the person causing it.
I lost all that I once made my gain.
All alone in sadness I now must sit.

Loving you was easy, losing you was hard.
Loving you is still easy,
but knowing you are no longer mine,
is the hardest of all.

Sometimes I wish I had never met you
because then I could go to bed at night
not knowing there was someone

LOVE: FROM THE DARKNESS TO THE LIGHT

like you out there.

I always knew looking back on the tears
would make me laugh,
but I never knew looking
back on the laughs would make me cry.

They say that if you love someone
you should let them go,
but they never say what to do
when they don't come back.

Having the love of your life
break up with you and saying
we can still be friends,
is like your dog dying and
your mom saying you can still keep it!

You always said you would be there,
that you would never leave me.
Well, now I need you more than ever
and all you can do is push me away

Real loss only occurs when you lose something
that you love more than yourself.
I don't know what to do now that we're apart;
I don't know how to live without the other half of my heart.

RAINBOW OF DEVOTION AND LOVE

"Thank you" are two words not used enough,
but I cry out with them to you so that
your kindness and caring spirit are heralded.

Dark clouds currently fill my life,
but there is hope for the cleansing waters

LOVE: FROM THE DARKNESS TO THE LIGHT

of falling rain that flow from your gentle soul.

May you see that the clouds of my mind
can be swept away with compassion from you,
so that I can offer you the treasures I have stored.

And may you know that all the storms raging
about you will pass as when you find someone to love,
a radiant rainbow will fill the horizon of your mind.

That rainbow will glisten and sparkle
because it proclaims the sanctity
and power found in true devotion and love.

MESSENGER OF LOVE

My love for you now only knows humility.
I steal into the alleys of darkness that surround me,
Longing to kiss one lock of your hair.
I cannot free myself, because I am your prisoner,
And I cannot break the chains that bind me.

I cannot love myself more than I love you.
I have died and can only be resurrected by you.
I have vanished from the horizon of hope without you.
I have sacrificed all my learning at the altar of faith for you.
Alas, I can only be a scholar by knowing love from you.
I have lost all my strength, but from you
Can come the power to enable me – yes, only from you.

I am your Knight in shining armour.
Come by my side and I will open the gate to paradise.
Come settle with ; we shall be neighbours with the stars.
You have been hiding for so long, drifting endlessly in
Stormy seas where my beacon of love cannot reach

LOVE: FROM THE DARKNESS TO THE LIGHT

You are connected to me as sure as the fetus is connected
To the mother by the umbilical cord of life.
Concealed, revealed into the unknown, un-manifested
You must reach out to embrace that which is within me.

You have been a wanderer in the wildness of love lost.
I will be your roaring ocean pounding the shore of hope.
Come merge with me and leave the world of doubt,
Ignorance and turmoil behind and move
Steadily toward the light of promise.

Be with me! Be with me! Be with me! Please be with me!
I will open the gate to promise and security.
I desire you more than I long for
the nourishment of food or drink.
I thirst and hunger like a lost soul for
one nod of hope from you.
My body, my senses, my mind long for your taste.
I can sense your over-powering presence in my heart.
Even if you are with another,
thinking it is rapturous contentment.
I wait with silent passion for
one gesture, one glance from you.

As I cry tears waiting for your acknowledgement,
I realize they are sacred raindrops from the heart.
They are not a mark of weakness, but of power.
They speak the words I cannot muster.
They speak more eloquently than 100,000 tongues.
The tears are messengers of my love.

AFFECTION IS A GREAT GIFT

My affection keeps growing
Like the flowers in the spring
And when they are fully opened

LOVE: FROM THE DARKNESS TO THE LIGHT

They are such a beautiful thing

My affection keeps growing
Between your heart and mine
Always staying connected
By the past's invisible twine

My affection keeps growing
Like the twinkling stars in the sky
Each day you hide coyly from me
As tears of loss form in my eyes

My affection keeps growing
Like the chirping of a singing bird
I know that my heart pounds
With your every spoken word

My affection keeps growing
And it gives me a soaring lift
If only you could somehow know
That my affection is a great gift

THE GIRL WHO CAN'T MAKE UP HER MIND

She vacillates,
turning to the one
she once loved.
"Oh, what do I do?"

How I long to help,
but reaching her
is frustration personified.
She makes my heart stir.

When he is on her mind,
She can't help herself.

LOVE: FROM THE DARKNESS TO THE LIGHT

Mentally naïve and physically promiscuous
Her hormones raging unabated.

She succumbs to temptation.
Actions manifest desire.
Gone is common sense
in a sea of infatuation.

Yet, there are times
when manipulation isn't there,
and she is mentally stable
and veils her emotions.

He sits on his throne
staining her mind,
knowing tears and pleas
solidify ignorance's key.

He cries "but I love you,"
To score his fake goal,
masking manipulation
as he captures her soul.

My heart palpitating with
reflections on what has been lost,
while hers beats with infatuation
that makes her pay a high cost.

If I believed in God,
I'd drop to my knees,
and just pray that his
manipulation she sees.

Can she analyze her life
and see it is filled with hope,
while people like me

LOVE: FROM THE DARKNESS TO THE LIGHT

struggle daily to cope.

She has the gold key,
but the dead bolt is in place,
because her infatuation is
what she must eventually face.

I want to see her happy.
That means the world to me.
If only she would open her eyes
and the truth finally see.

THE GREAT PRETENDER

I am going to be a pretender
The rest of my life.
If I ever kiss a girl again,
I will pretend it is her.
If I ever sleep with a girl again,
I will pretend it is her.
If I ever have another relationship,
I will pretend it is with her.
If I ever get engaged,
I will pretend I am engaged to her.
If I ever get married,
I will pretend I am marrying her.
If I have children,
I will pretend the children are hers and mine.
Everything will be a lie the rest of my life.
I shall be the Great Pretender.

THE BLUE CAR

I look out my window and wait,
Another day battling my fate.

LOVE: FROM THE DARKNESS TO THE LIGHT

Where is that old blue car
That brings my love from afar?

I need to see her so bad.
Goddamn, I am so sad.
I want her to just care.
That would ease my fear.

Our life was like a leaping stream,
where sweet aromas rose and trembled,
but sometimes a dark cloud would appear
and slowly devour the sun.

I remember those gifts from the earth:
indelible scents, gold clay,
but there were weeds in the thicket
penetrating thorns like swords.

But I fondly remember
the bouquets we picked,
the shadows and silent water,
like a foam-covered stone.

That time was like never, and like always.
So I go there, but she is not waiting.
Where is that goddamn blue car?
That brings my love from afar.

FROM ACROSS A CROWDED ROOM AGAIN

I once wrote a poem of love
Of how across a crowded room I saw a maiden so fair.
I sang of her sweetness and how I pinned for her,
Even though she appeared not to even know I was there.

I whispered to God on high,

LOVE: FROM THE DARKNESS TO THE LIGHT

"Life would be wonderful and pure
To spend eternity with this fair maiden,"
But I was shy and unsure.

The poem I wrote told of how
The sanguine thought of that night never left my mind.
Burned into my soul was that smile.
Pounding heart had I, as I longed for she who was so fine.

Fate is a livid hunter of hope, so I found her again.
That time I conquered my fear.
And nervously whispered "hello"
To this vision so lovely and dear.

That classic smile crept across her face,
And her eyes lit up like stars so bright.
"I remember you," she said so softly.
"You stared at me across a crowded room one night."

Ah, we came together in what I thought was bliss.
For 20 years I assumed our love was in full bloom
Each day I would fondly remember
Seeing her from across a crowded room.

But the lamp had flickered and nearly died,
Without me being aware of what I had done.
She is gone now with another.
Yet, still into her arms I want to run.

I look at what was and what could have been.
I am shamefully unaware of any pain I caused.
Yet, I plead for an opportunity to make recompense.
But, enamoured with a new lover, her heart has paused.

I stare at four walls and pace the floor.
I never realized I was destined for doom.

LOVE: FROM THE DARKNESS TO THE LIGHT

Oh, how I wish once again I could go to place of mirth,
And see her smiling from across a crowded room.

A BOON FROM HE WHO REMEMBERS
YOU SO WELL

Outside my window I hear the gentle breeze,
As it caresses the leaves from the tall trees,
And carries them flittering all around,
Then they gently fall upon the ground.

I see the birds so high above,
Their songs chirping of love.
And laid upon their soft sweet wing
My affection for you they bring.

And as they start their graceful descent,
Delivering a message that's serenely sent,
I want you to know to me you are so dear
And I forlornly wish you were near.

Upon your soft breast I would lay my weary head,
Letting my affection upon you spread.
A day has never passed without thoughts of you.
Ah, how many times did I miss your cue?

The ravages of time can shake me to the core,
But a golden moment with you would make my spirits soar.
I can now do that which I wanted for so long,
But circumstance prevented me from singing the song.

Is it too late
For us to finally welcome fate?
True devotion and affection we cannot fight.
I think now is time for us to see the light.

———

LOVE: FROM THE DARKNESS TO THE LIGHT

A PLEA TO MARIE LAVEAU

With my love I went to see
where Marie Laveau's bones lay in repose.
The grave is now covered with
water from the mighty Ponchatrain.
Those days with my lover I knew no pain.

Looking at where she lay,
I held my lover's hand and
discussed the black magic
of the voodoo queen.
Our happiness was easily seen.

How I wish I could resurrect the queen,
and plead for a spell she could
stitch when my lover sleeps.
Ah, a hex she would weave
To make my lover to me cleave.

She threads her hexes with heat,
blue fire flaring from her fingertips.
Ah a spell, a spell that is what I need
from the voodoo queen Marie Laveau.
Because the one I love has laid me low.

ONE MORE TIME

I miss you on Friday.
I miss you on Saturday.
Without you I am so blue.
You're like a dream come true

I was just a face you noticed long ago
From across a crowded room.
Now I'm just trying to be honest and pure.

LOVE: FROM THE DARKNESS TO THE LIGHT

With myself, with you, as I seek the cure.

You might think that I'm a fool
For falling over you,
So tell me what I can do to prove
That it's not so hard to do?

Give love a try, one more time
'Cause you know that I'm on your side
Give love a try, one more time
In me you can confide.

How did it play out with Bogie and Bacall?
She to his heart had the key.
Only you can unlock my mind.
That is so easy to see.

Your eyes, when I saw them for the first time,
I knew that I was going love you for all time
With a love so real, so right.
Even when you are out of sight.

You might think that I'm a fool
For pining so much over you,
So tell me what I can do to prove myself
As it is all I am asking to do?

Give our love a try one more time.
Because you know that I'm on your side
Give our love a try one more time
Please, one more time – just one more time.

COME AND GET IT

Ignoring my impassioned pleas,
She tries to help by asking for cheese.

LOVE: FROM THE DARKNESS TO THE LIGHT

I walk up and down in pain that she
cannot understand or even see.

I am alone and my heart stayed.
My spirit is shredded and flayed.
While she is in the arms of another,
Who makes her heart flutter.

Watching them in domestic bliss
makes me just remember what I miss.
She cannot see around the bend.
She thinks my pain will eventually end.

I have died but am not buried.
So her love by me is still curried.
My years of devotion are ignored,
As by her I am deplored.

The hope fades further each day I am sure,
As for my broken heart there is only one cure.
She holds the key to make me whole,
But she chooses to crush my soul.

So a grilled cheese is supposed to ease the pain.
Ah, I think how impertinent and lame.
Yet, that is the way she shows compassion today.
With cascading tears "come and get it" I say.

Quote: Love is blind and often unkind.

I WILL LOVE YOU UNTIL THE END OF TIME

You fit me better than a glove
I know that love is mean, and love hurts
But I still remember that day we met in October.
I will love you 'til the end of time

LOVE: FROM THE DARKNESS TO THE LIGHT

I would wait a hundred years,
And still love you more
Than those you embrace now.
I love you more than those bastards before.
Say you'll remember, say you'll remember
I will love you until the end of time

You left to start your life over
I was crying, "No please, stay here,
We can make it work,"
But you headed out the door,
I stayed up waiting, anticipating, and pacing.
I will love you until the end of time
I would wait a hundred years
Promise you'll remember that you're mine
I cannot see through my tears

I told you that no matter what you did I'd be by your side,
Because without you I will die,
Yet, you left on the fly.
Well damn, give me one more try.
When you walked out that door, a piece of me died.
I told you I would give you more,
But I cannot reach that calculating mind.
I promised it would not be like before.

You boldly and coldly walked out of my life.
You just need to remember....
I will love you until the end of time.
I would wait a hundred years.
Promise you'll remember that you're mine.
I cannot see through the tears.
I love you more
Than those you embrace now.
Say you'll remember; say you'll remember.
I will love you until the end of time.

LOVE: FROM THE DARKNESS TO THE LIGHT

FRESH AIR

Don't really know what to say.
Life is complex and so am I (I think).
Sometimes, I look at life like a house.
It can be really comfy.
Sometimes it gets cold and you need to turn on the heat.
Sometimes, it's too warm and you can't breathe.
So you just need to open a window.
And that's basically why I long for you.
I simply need a bit of fresh air.

FINDING THE BLUEBIRD

Aaron Adams fell to is knees
burned out by love as if it was a disease.
He could not fathom the depth of his despair
as he traversed the murderer's lair.
He meandered through the corridors of fire
in his private hell, and he remembered a song
that Charlie Manson used to sing in his cell,
or was it Marilyn Manson he thought,
as he reached up and pulled the fire alarm
to alert the authorities that he had finally
cornered the murderer.
Yes, he had found the one who killed
John Marley and Denise Dorman.
Yet, Aaron had been murdered, too, without knowing it.
His heart had been cut out,
because there was a hollowness in him now,
a hollowness that time would never heal.

Charlie Manson sang the song in his cell.
Then Marilyn Manson rang the alarm bell.
Asking if the world was really round,
And where the blue bird of happiness might be found.

LOVE: FROM THE DARKNESS TO THE LIGHT

We all want to know why the sky above is so blue.
When you were a child did anyone tell you?
What becomes of the sun when it falls into the sea?
And who lights it again as bright as it can be?
Why can no one fly without wings in the skies?
Why are there so many tears in people's eyes?

Charlie Manson sang the song in his cell.
Then Marilyn Manson rang the alarm bell.
Yes, yes, it is true the world is really round.
And the bluebird may one day be found.
And the sky up above may be so blue and clear,
So that you'll see the bluebird if it should appear.
And the sun doesn't fall when it slips out of sight.
All it does is make way for the moon's pretty light.
And if we could fly there would be no need for birds.
And people cry, because they are touched by words.

Charlie Manson sang the song in his cell.
Then Marilyn Manson rang the alarm bell.
Don't be sad if it's true the world's round.
Search everywhere until the bluebird is found.
But there is no need to wander very far.
For what you really seek is where you are.
Show me some love and here is what I will do.
I will take the dear bluebird and give it to you.
Put the bluebird's love in your heart pure and true,
So heaven will once again bless me with you.

HARK, HARK, HUSH AND HARK

Hush, hark, hush and hark!
You left he whom you once loved
And embraced another who imprisoned you.
So, you think that you cannot escape from
The winsome sorrowful cry

LOVE: FROM THE DARKNESS TO THE LIGHT

Of the wind in the dark
Blown by the new warden of your heart.
Hush, hark, hush and hark,
Without a murmur or sigh,
Bow not your head in dismay.
Shed that harsh thread
That binds you to servitude.
Cut lose he who restrains,
Manipulates, cajoles and imprisons.
Hush, hark, hush and hark!

Open the door.
Listen. Listen.
Hush, hark, hush and hark.
It is the wind's muffled roar,
And the glistening
Of tears round the moon.
And in sweet fancy, the thread
Of misery can be snapped.
You can free yourself now
From him whose ego you satisfied
And stroked so delicately.
There is a vanishing swoon
Out of the night.
Be free of your shackles!
Hush, hark, hush and hark.

REMBERING THE GREAT PRETENDER

I remember an old song my mother listened to.
She even sang along as she moved about the house.
I now am sadly humming it myself,
Because within me there is a fire I cannot douse.

Oh yes I am the great pretender.
Pretending I am doing well.

LOVE: FROM THE DARKNESS TO THE LIGHT

My need is such I pretend too much.
I am so lonely but few can tell.

Oh yes, I am the great pretender.
Adrift in a world of my own.
I play the game but to my shame.
You've left me to dream all alone.

You are with another and you do not pretend.
You are gay and carefree like a clown.
While I am nursing a broken heart,
Because you are no longer around.

In my heart there is something I cannot conceal.
My spirit is in shambles, broken and torn.
I sometimes pretend that you are still around.
But I just get more forlorn.

My mother sang it so well long ago.
Now, all I can do is wear a frown.
Yes I am the great pretender.
Pretending you are still around.

HOPE'S BRIGHT LIGHT

She loves me, but she loves another more.
Will she forever close affection's open door?
My cries of anguish she elected to ignore.
Ah, where does she want to go for evermore?

She now fears sickness of heart.
She fears being lost in the dark.
She fears the loss of that
Which lit love's spark.

She fears the unknown.

LOVE: FROM THE DARKNESS TO THE LIGHT

Her fear is something new,
As inside webs of lost hope are sown.
She fears that her lovers are few.

That fear throttles hope
And brings forgotten pain
That played for so many
Years in such a stupid game.

She fears the future
For what it may hold.
The fear inside her is part
of the result of growing old.

Yet, I have my hand out
To clasp her in an embrace,
Because I now see her as
Delicate as fine Belgium lace.

I shall light for her a candle
To guide her through the night,
For I am her beacon who wants
To shine hope's bright light.

I AM NOTHING

In my heart you were once there
to fill a deep void.
I felt you, all the time, everywhere.
Now you are absent, and I am empty.
Frantically needing you,
I am crying in the wilderness of despair.
Only you can bring a little joy.
I wish I could be strong
and emotionally aloof like you.
But I am weak when

LOVE: FROM THE DARKNESS TO THE LIGHT

not loved by you.
I wish you would reach out to me.
I need you to understand and see
without you, I am nothing.

THE ROARING FIRE OF LOVE

If I was any kind of a man,
I would go to her lover
and sweep her into my arms and shrilly say,
"She is mine and I will fight for her."
Then I would usher her out the door,
put her in the car and drive away,
claiming my prize of love.
Alas, I am not a man,
only a broken shell that is hollow inside.
She abides in his arms
while I sit idly by, counting flowers on the wall.
And it does not bother her at all.
Or, does it? Is there within her
just one spark left from the old embers?
Will she let the embers sizzle and crackle
until they build into a roaring fire again?

> Saying goodbye is sometimes easier than saying hello.

GOODBYE IS MY WORST FEAR

My days draw long and weary,
when you are no longer here.
Confidence is filled with questions,
strength replaced by fear.

The assuredness that I woke with each day,
is no longer to be found,
As though my dreams and aspirations,

LOVE: FROM THE DARKNESS TO THE LIGHT

were buried under ground.

I hear your voice being carried by the wind,
and sense your fingers run through my non-existent hair.
I close my eyes and remember your kiss,
and wish that you were here.

So with nothing left but one thing to say,
to resolve my heart break here.
Don't say good-bye my darling and my love,
Good-bye is my worst fear.

HE STOPPED LOVING HER

*In my pain, I am reminded of
what I have done wrong.
And suddenly, I think of
the George Jones song*

He said I'll love you 'til I die.
She told him you'll forget in time.
As the years went slowly by
She still preyed upon his mind.

*Those lines remind me of our commitment
To one another to endure through better or worse.
Yet, it is I who have all the pain.
And now she thinks me insane.*

He kept her picture on his wall;
Went half crazy now and then.
He still loved her through it all,
Hoping she'd come back again.

*Those lines bring sadness to the mind.
Making it impossible to survive*

LOVE: FROM THE DARKNESS TO THE LIGHT

In a crazy state of pain,
Knowing her heart I might not gain.

He kept some letters by his bed
Dated 1994.
He had underlined in red
every single I love you.

My life began in 1994,
And it may have ended in 2013,
When she walked away.
Oh, if only she would stay.

I went to see him just today.
Oh, but I didn't see no tears.
All dressed up to go away;
First time I'd seen him smile in years.

Those lines remind me that my smile is gone.
The tears spill like falling rain.
There is nowhere for me to go.
My spirits are so low.

He stopped loving her today.
They placed a wreath upon his door,
And soon they'll carry him away.
He stopped loving her today.

COME HOME TO ME

Come home to me, this is all my heart will ask.
Come home to me, let's put our disagreements in the past.
Come home to me, we'll forgive all
and turn everything around,
I need to hear your sweet tender sound.
Come home to me, let our hearts be as one together,

LOVE: FROM THE DARKNESS TO THE LIGHT

Come home to me, separate our love again never.
Come home to me, allow me to love you with all my heart.
Come home to me, and do not stay apart.
Come home to me, let our lives pick up
and start where we went wrong.
Come home to me, let's lead our lives
from the beginning like they were meant to be.
Come home to me, I've loved you so long,
now I need you to love me.
Come home baby, please I beg of you,
Come home baby, let me prove
my love will always be true.
Come home to me, that is all I desire,
but now I know it is not enough.
Come home to me even thou
the emptiness will always be there.
Come home to me, even though I have lost all hope.
Come home to me, even though
we cannot make things as they were.
Come home to me even though
there is a divide which cannot be breeched.
Come home to me even though the misery will not fade.
Come home to me so I can at least look
at you and remember what once was.
Come home to me because I had rather
be miserable with you than miserable without you.
Come home to me! Please come home to me.
Come home to me!

BEFORE I MET YOU

I saw you in my dreams before I met you.
I kissed you before I knew you,
I loved you before I saw the light.
We are never given the power
to dream without also being given the power

LOVE: FROM THE DARKNESS TO THE LIGHT

to make them come true.
In a blink of an eye,
my dreams became reality,
but what I didn't see
was that you would leave me.

THE RHYTHM OF LOVE

May you find great peace and comfort
in the bosom of your family on this holiday,
and maybe just find a small memory somewhere
within of he who has been devoted to you for 20 years.
I longed to hear from you yesterday
to assuage my aching heart
and ease the loneliness that entraps me,
but I know that the ties that bind us
are unravelled a little more each day by you,
as you seek a life free of me.
I miss so much those holidays
when I shared life with you.
Now I dread the arrival of a holiday,
because I must endure the loneliness of lost hope.
I shall die with your name on my lips
as the dark clouds of eternity surround me
and finally free me of the pain.
Thank you for allowing me 20 years of ecstasy
that shall forever rest, protected and revered,
in a corner of my heart that still beats
with the rhythm of love for you.

A DEBT I CAN NEVER REPAY

You were a star that shined brightly
in the dark skies that surrounded me.
That star seeped through my veins
and became a part of me.

LOVE: FROM THE DARKNESS TO THE LIGHT

And then I had to put it back into the sky.
That was the most painful thing I have had to do in my life.
However, even though it's up in the sky
and shining on someone else now,
I still feel its warmth coursing through my body.

As I walk about in a daze,
I have sweet recollections of the woman
who left a map in my mind,
because everywhere I am,
every time I am alone or in a crowd,
I have thoughts of you and through silent tears
I recall the deep, abiding memories of the days
when I went on wonderful journeys with you
and felt a part of your life
and sensed that you cared about me
almost as much as I cared about you.

My gratefulness for the time you shared with me transcends
all else in my life of quiet desperation.
Your once great love for me
that is now reserved for another,
sustains me through memories of what once was.
I owe you a debt I can never repay.
My heart is bankrupt with pain,
but the mere sight of you
brings back the breath of life
that now is smothered in pain without you.

THE GOLDEN THREAD

The time I spend with you is like a golden thread
sewing hope on a worn out piece of cloth.
The thread is all that holds the garment together.
You are the thread and I am the tattered garment.
An old worn out garment can sparkle and shine

LOVE: FROM THE DARKNESS TO THE LIGHT

when the golden thread coarsens through it.
Without the thread, it should just
be tossed into the trash, because it has no usefulness
and offers no beauty to the world.

MUSIC OF LOVE

The music of love must be played by two.
It is not a solo performance.
You must push all the right buttons to bring life to love.
When a heart breaks, that is
when you find whether there is real love or not.
When the cold storm of the world
blows winds of discontent
that is when you must find that sunlight together
that will shine with the soft reflection
of the divine radiance of love.

THE LIGHT OF DAY

Stop being a victim is easy to say.
She tells me things will be OK.
Yet, she doesn't feel my dismay.
As in misery I despondently lay

'Just get over it,' they say
I wish I could find a way
Living with it day by day
Memories won't go away

Medication helped to sway
Many feelings of dismay
As her love began to decay
And the map of hurt I did survey.

Show me the way

LOVE: FROM THE DARKNESS TO THE LIGHT

I want to be OK
But here I forlornly lay,
Begging for the light of day.

I MISS YOU

There once again is that feeling of loneliness
coming from deep down inside,
Being without you causes such a hurt,
A feeling I can not seem to hide.
They say there's a silver lining
to every dark cloud in the sky,
Finding the lining to my cloud
would be to look you in the eye.
Each night I lay my head down on the bed to rest,
My love for you I cannot resist.
Making decisions, trying to figure out
how to live without you
Figuring out what I should do,
Never gets easier as I still long for you.
I believe in your heart you still care for me
I missed you the minute I drew out of your sight,
I Love You, Sweet Dreams, and Good Night.

CLOSING LOVE'S DOOR

There is a truth that I learned yesterday.
It came as I pondered in my bed where I lay.
Misjudged, upset, and wounded, I stayed.
My lover said things, she should not say.
They stood in my mind and the pain increased.
She tried to offer solace, it gave no release.
Imposing expectations and misplaced demands.
I thought, "She must change, to receive my hand!"
The day then passed, I knew she was not fair.
My hurt was simply too hard to bear.

LOVE: FROM THE DARKNESS TO THE LIGHT

Through reconciliation, I sought relief
Hoping that time would heal my grief.
And then when humility, finally obliged.
Through tears I tried to wipe out the deep hurt inside.
My eyes still see clearly, my lover's intent.
I want to move on and sever hopelessness I lament.
Forgive me my pain, for the hurt is like a sin.
Oh, my tormented soul wants to be free again.
Go away hurt, go away please I need to move on,
But there is something, something that is now gone.
I cry inside as I know she does not love me as before.
Please I am so lonely now that she has closed love's door.

WHERE LONELINESS DWELLS

Experience has taught me well
As in a valley of sorrow and loneliness
I forlornly and miserably dwell.
Ah, what I would give for her kiss.
Long ago now into lost hope I fell.
It is her smile, her softness I miss.

No matter how hard I try
Each day a little I die.
Hope is gone from my life,
As it is filled with strife.
The sun no longer shines,
Because on my heart sorrow dines.
Welcome to where loneliness dwells.

TARRY NOT – SEIZE THE DAY

When you are old and grey and full of sleep,
And nodding by the fire, take down my book,
And slowly read, and dream of the soft look
My eyes had for you, and of their shadows deep.

LOVE: FROM THE DARKNESS TO THE LIGHT

Of how I loved your moments of glad grace,
And loved your beauty of soul deep and true,
Of how I wanted to sexually embrace you,
And loved the sweetness of your lovely face;

And bending down beside the glowing ember bars,
Murmur, a little sadly, how quickly time fled
And paced upon the mountains overhead
And hid its face amid a crowd of stars.

There is so little time that youth cannot understand,
But when you are old and your hair flecked with grey,
Remember the time when I wanted but did not demand,
And in my cold dark grave my desires will sadly lay.

You lit up a cloudy sky with a smile of hope,
Within me the fires of passion you did provoke.
We had sweet serenity where we quietly lay,
Ah, passion should always seize the day.

FOREVER GONE

In loneliness, pining for her love, I await a sign.
She said I would adjust and forget her in time.
I tried so hard but it just won't work.
How I wish each day she was by my side.
Oh, the things in her I used to confide.

Will this loneliness ever fade?
Can I ever accept the decision she made?
My dreams have faded into darkness.
It is I who gets all the blame.
But I am now not the same.

The love I have causes so much pain.
And she just keeps telling me I'm insane.

LOVE: FROM THE DARKNESS TO THE LIGHT

Oh, if some how she would pull me near.
How I want to watch the flowers bloom.
But all I can see is my dismal gloom.

They say misery loves company, so I search.
There are others like me, on a precarious perch.
But their pain cannot assuage mine.
Oh, how I treasure her as I sit alone.
But I know that she is forever gone.

WHEN I'M HURTING

It's easier for you to walk away,
than it is for you to reach out to me.
It's easier for you to look away,
than it is for you to see the depth of my despair.
It's easier for you to look through me,
than it is for you to see "me."
It's easier for you to distance yourself,
than it is for you to really care.
It's easier for you to hear,
than it is for you to listen.
It's easier for you to judge,
than it is for you to understand.
It's easier for you to label,
than it is to get acquainted.
It's easier for you to bask in your joy,
than it is for you to feel my pain.
It's easier for you to be bewildered at my mysteries,
than it is for you to probe deeply into the depths of my soul.

It's easier for me to look away,
than to let you see the feelings betrayed through my eyes.
It's easier for me to cry,
than it is for me to talk.
It's easier for me to walk alone,

LOVE: FROM THE DARKNESS TO THE LIGHT

than it is to risk rejection.
It's easier for me to push you away,
than it is for me to be held.
It's easier for me to distance myself,
than it is to trust that you won't hurt me.
It's easier for me to die,
than it is for me to face life's challenges.

It's hard for me to smile
when I am hurting.
It's hard for me to talk
when you won't understand.
It's hard for me to reach out
when I need help the most.

If only you'd really look at me
and see who I am.
If only you cared enough to reach out
when I push you away.
If only you'd hold me,
without asking why.
If only you'd acknowledge
the validity of my feelings.
But it's the easy roads that are most often taken.
And so I hurt alone.

YOU MURDERED ME

You murdered me.
Murdered me for what you thought was love.
Murder that was covered up with unmitigated lies.
You committed murder as I looked in your eyes.

You tell me over and over you still love me,
But what you do only shows love for another,
You are committing my murder in the third degree.

LOVE: FROM THE DARKNESS TO THE LIGHT

My love for you will simply never let me be free.

THE PAIN I CAUSED HER

I loved her but knew not what I was doing to her.
She was the right person for me,
But I did not know I was the wrong person for her.
I created a relationship that was hollow,
Blinded by belief in my own goodness toward her.
How much I loved and adored but still bit like a serpent.
I could not see the wounds that were afflicting her.
I did not realize I was throwing stones in her path,
Which she then used to build a wall around her.
I was the architect of my own doom,
As I erected a monument to stupidity that broke her.
She was defined by the light she wanted to shine.
She was my salvation but I was too stupid to see it in her.
I knew the price of everything,
But not the cost of what she thought I did to her.
I thought I had a brilliant mind,
But my heart should have heard the silent pain in her.
Anger swelled and she had vindictiveness,
And it worked faster than my mind with her.
I did not realize that I was drowning myself in agony,
When I should have been realizing the hurt within her.
She felt like her ship was sinking,
And there was no lifejacket for her.
She discarded that which was weighing her down,
And I was the chief impediment to her.
She followed her heart to free herself from me.
If only she could know that I am dead without her.
I know I need to let her go for her happiness,
But I fight the loss of life within because I need her.
Yet, I cannot believe that we were together by accident.
There was a deep, abiding reason why I found her.
How I wish she could look at the good in me,

LOVE: FROM THE DARKNESS TO THE LIGHT

And realize that my love never wavered for her.
I know she looks upon me as a pariah,
And I am a colossal failure to her.
I wallow in deep misery with my affliction.
I just want to know that I am still something to her.
How I wish that I could make amends for my sins,
And shout I am sorry for the pain I might have caused her.

SHE SLIPPED AWAY

The first night we met
I knew it to be true
This girl standing before me
Was genuine and true.

I looked into your eyes.
The deep browns didn't lie
You loved me so very much
I knew by your soft sigh.

The nights turned into mornings.
The days went by far too quick.
My sickness let the love slip away,
As it was just impossible to lick.

Then finally the day had come
You said you couldn't wait.
Time had passed so swiftly.
Now, it was far too late.

It was then I realized
I made a huge mistake.
I let the girl I loved
Simply slip away, simply slip away.

Love's dying embers crackle and smoulder in loneliness.

LOVE: FROM THE DARKNESS TO THE LIGHT

SANITY'S FADING LIGHT

When you love someone
who doesn't love you back,
when you've given so much
of your mind, body and soul
and you long for her to care,
the hurt is your greatest fear.

When she is all you think about
be it morning, midday or night,
the hurt sears deep within
and scorches your soul.
How you long for that which was,
but now in her has taken pause.

When she doesn't call or e-mail
you spend another lonely night
in the despair of lost hope.
The pain and hurt bypasses your heart
and cuts deep into your soul
where it festers dark like a clump of coal.

You think of that other man
who now has captured her heart.
You cannot understand how she
can love someone so dark.
Why doesn't this woman understand
that she has put you in a barren land?

When you have cried a river of tears,
given your all and cursed your fate,
when you realize it is just too late,
when you have apologized, begged
pleaded and supplicated yourself in despair,
you finally realize that life is not fair.

LOVE: FROM THE DARKNESS TO THE LIGHT

When you ride that roller coaster of emotion
with all its ups and downs and you
are depressed and angry at yourself
for loving her so much it hurts,
you look back on the mirth you had
and try hard not to be so sad.

Strolling through the streets of agony,
You know what is forever gone.
There is no hope now to recover
That which has been so sorrowfully lost.
Deep within you pray for the end
As no hope can anyone lend.

IN SILENCE

Where once the sounds of lovers' hearts pounded,
Now sit silent and empty rooms.
The oak floors creak as if embracing loneliness.
Wishful thoughts of a rumbled bed,
Ah, midnight fantasies in my head.

In frenzied haste our clothes we would shed.
Sweet memories, but alas there is only silence now.
The gaiety is gone with broken pieces of hearts.
Our paths cross now and then, but our time is gone.
She says love dissipated, so I am alone.

We had our time in glorious euphoria,
but now there is silence.
How can storied silence be so infernally deafening?
The season of our discontent descended upon us in a cloud,
As the time of radiant blooming passed into winter frost.
In between, lived happiness, but now in silence it is lost.

> The beacon of love shines but can dim.

LOVE: FROM THE DARKNESS TO THE LIGHT

WHAT COULD HAVE BEEN

Without you I am as sad
as a bird without wings,
a lion without a roar,
a violin with one string,
a piano with no keys.
Mine is a solitary journey
to the inner reaches of loneliness and despair.
There is no respite from the longing
for that which is now impossible.
You have doused the flame,
and the fire only smoulders
with memories of what once was,
and what could have been.

DON'T BE AFRAID

Don't be afraid to jump into uncertainty.
How will you know what is waiting for you,
If you don't step into the dark in search of light?
If fear overtakes you when you begin to wrestle with life,
Remember without that first step,
You cannot move forward?
Move with assuredness to embrace your potential.
You never have to fear,
Because just as I always have been,
I am here to give you support
And protect you from harm.

DEVOTION IN A CUP OF AFFECTION

My life has been a mosaic of adventures
of the mind, body and soul.
However, I now have no one
to share my life with.

LOVE: FROM THE DARKNESS TO THE LIGHT

A life not shared is a life of shallowness.
If you have no one to lavish attention on,
what is the use of getting up every day.
Doing for oneself does not bring the joy
that comes from watching that special someone smile
with delight at the little things that whisper "I love you"
in ways that are not measured not in the amount spent
but in the amount of devotion that is poured
into the cup of affection.

THE SCARF OF DISCONTENT

My life is now like a book filled with tragedy.
I read over and over hoping for a happy ending.
Trees of fall lie at angles in my mind,
Felled by a winter storm of discontent,
And she whom I love so dearly
prepares merrily and gaily for
Cold weather far from me in the arms of another.

November light slants through the oaks of my mind
As a parade of lost hope passes in the psyche,
Sloshing along with the winter wind
Searching treetops for the last leaf
To steal from the tree of life.
The past love lies on the forest floor,
Not evergreen but oaken,
Its branches latched to a greying sky
as I die more each day.

Ah, and now her winter scarves are gone with her,
and in their place she left a scathing bookmark.
It is a mark that says she will never return
to explore what we knew and did not know.
Oh, we knew once in the spreading twilight
love that is now a flowing scarf of discontent for me.

LOVE: FROM THE DARKNESS TO THE LIGHT

CALAMITY OF THE MIND

The coming storm blackens the sky of the mind.
It threatens sanity, lucidity and happiness
Like a black shroud of doom, covering every thing.
It is as if there is something lurking within me,
Waiting to destroy all my hopes and dreams.
I am swept up in the torrents of wind that blow with
A clammy coldness warning of a coming calamity.
Contentment is shattered by fear of that which awaits
In the darkness of my own unsure mind.

I'VE LOVED YOU FOR SO LONG

You come to me a bit forlorn today.
Oh, how I want to embrace you my dear.
You had so much to sadly say.
And I want to quiet your fear.
Why can't you once again love me
When I've loved you for so long?
Perhaps you could just try to see
That I am part of your sweet song.
I might bring smiles to fill your days,
And words to fit your songs.
If only you would come and stay.
I've loved you for so long.
Vainly, you search elsewhere to find
The love you ever seek.
Touch and take this love of mine,
A love that's yours to keep.

THE FLAME FLICKERED

There was a time when the flame never flickered.
It burned like a pigeon's feet on a hot tin roof.
The eyes were glazed with passion.

LOVE: FROM THE DARKNESS TO THE LIGHT

The touch exuded warmth that penetrated the soul.

How he remembered that first embrace.
Arousal deep within made him gasp for breath.
Her soft demeanour made his heart flutter
as if given the key to eternal grace.

The time together was like a ripening grape
on an ethereal vine in the bright, warm sun.
The wine, aged with love, flowed into a
cornucopia of passion for each lover's sake.

As the years passed, a cold wind from afar
seemed to doom them to an exorable fate.
Recriminations seemed to crop up at every turn,
constantly their attachment to mar.

Why did the flame flicker,
that was once so bright?
Why were they doomed to see the
end of that bright, penetrating light?

The days passed with a silence sublime.
The warmth of a touch a distant memory.
That gaze of love no longer shined in the eyes.
The words spoken were never kind.

The flame went low and flickered away.
To be snuffed out for eternity,
It can never be rekindled, because the harsh words
Destroyed the loving serenity.

Looking back on his attempts to reconcile,
He knows he tried his best.
But, it takes two to make things work.
So, the flame flickered and died at her behest.

LOVE: FROM THE DARKNESS TO THE LIGHT

CHRISTMAS PAIN

She is missing this Christmas,
one place at table of love is bare,
one smiling face I will yearn for
just knowing you are not there.

Voice soft and diminished,
I sing no Christmas song,
my life is on hold
for you have been gone so long.

The joy of your sweet laughter
as at the piano we gathered around.
Your spirit was like 'Peter Pan'
in revelry and melodic sound.

Cozy by a crackling fire
I will surely quietly sit,
recalling times past
when we both sit in front of it.

I have to gather all my strength
and be of one accord in my darkness.
Knowing you are with another
does not make me love you any less.

ALL MY MIGHT AT CHRISTMAS

I miss you at Christmas.
I am lonely without you.
My heart aches with memories,
As they come into view.

I think of the times we shared
I never dreamed I would be without you.

LOVE: FROM THE DARKNESS TO THE LIGHT

But now the bell tolls for me as
I am one of those forgotten few.

You have chosen a new life over me.
Take it up and remember I am here;
Therefore you are still in my heart
Where I protect you from fear.

Light a candle and watch the flame
Flicker all about with dancing delight,
And know this special day I am here
And still love you with all my might.

MALICIOUS EVIL

One who was wrapped in infatuation and lust
Stood in awe looking up at what he had lost.
He could not see he was better
for being free of her.
She was sitting on the throne of wickedness,
Sipping the dark wine
of vain, destructive malevolence.
She was drunk with her
own beastly, depraved villainy.
She was a woman arrayed in purple and scarlet,
And adorned with jewels
and pearls of maliciousness.
She held the cup of abominations and impurities.
She was the epitome of malignant, malicious evil.
Ah, but he was dreaming, wishing it was so,
Because that would make it easier to let go.

MISERY WITHOUT YOU

The was a bright star that shone for awhile
in the dark skies that surrounded me.

LOVE: FROM THE DARKNESS TO THE LIGHT

That star seeped through my veins
and became a part of me.
And then I had to put it back into the sky.
That was the most painful thing
I have had to do in my life.
However, even though it's up in the sky
and shining on someone else now,
I still feel its warmth coursing through my body.

As I walk about in a daze,
I have sweet recollections of the woman
who left a map in my mind,
because everywhere I am,
every time I am alone or in a crowd
I have thoughts of you and through silent tears
I recall the deep, abiding memories of the days
when I went on wonderful journeys with you
and felt a part of your life
and sensed that you cared about me
almost as much as I cared about you.

My gratefulness for the time
you shared with me transcends
all else in my life of quiet desperation.
The great love you faked for me
is now reserved for another.
I am sustained by memories of what once was.
I owe you a debt I can never repay.
My heart is bankrupt with pain,
but the mere sight of you
brings back the breath of life
that now is smothered in misery without you.

WELCOME TO HELL

The sign outside the dilapidated hotel

LOVE: FROM THE DARKNESS TO THE LIGHT

Should have read, welcome to hell.
This was the last stop on the way to nowhere.
The people there had bought a one way ticket
To life lived in the abyss of self-doubt.
This was the cellar of misery far beyond belief,
And from its bowels there simply was no relief.

Scoring another drink was their life
These agonizing poor souls were lost in strife.
There lives had been tossed to the wayward wind,
They longed for death to bring the pain to an end.
Within the corridors there is a lonely forlorn cry.
They long for a hand up from the pain,
But nobody will play the compassion game.

Looking all about the wasteland of lost hope,
Dignity has taken a long, undeserved holiday.
How many there would sell their soul for one sip?
The fountain of hope is dry in this place.
These people could simply not keep pace.
Yes, the sign outside should read welcome to hell.
Where hope, opportunity, charity, benevolence,
And compassion do not dwell.

THE ILL WIND OF DESPAIR

The coming storm blackens the sky of the mind.
It threatens sanity, lucidity and happiness
Like a black shroud of doom, covering every thing.
It is as if there is something lurking within,
Waiting to destroy all hopes and dreams,
Sweeping them up in the torrents
Of whirling winds that blow with
A clammy coldness warning of a coming calamity.
Contentment is shattered by fear of that
Which lurks in dark corners and awaits

LOVE: FROM THE DARKNESS TO THE LIGHT

> In the murkiness of an unsure irresolute mind.
> Hope darkens and the ill wind of despair blows
> With fear, making one tremble with trepidation.

As I often do when suffering great pain, I turn to writing in order to pour out my soul and relieve some of the hurt through prose. After my wife left me, I wrote two books where my famous detective, Aaron Adams had to deal with the pain f losing his wife. It was a cathartic experience that afforded me the opportunity to use my sorrow in a creative way. Thus, the below excerpt from THE GIRL WHO SAID GOODBYE FOR THE LAST TIME is the result of the pain I was feeling.

During Aaron's early struggles, Jasmine had not even been born, but in 1963, on the day she entered the world of sorrow that had already engulfed Aaron, the sun, no doubt, gave off a special twinkle, signifying the arrival of an angel who would walk the earth reaching out with kindness and compassion to all who crossed her path in this too often sorrowful journey called life. She was vintage wine that had cooled and long aged in the deep-delved earth. Jasmine was dance, song and sun burnt mirth. The bubbles of hope beaded with effervescence, reaching to the brim with the gaiety of a world filled with possibilities rather than hopelessness.

> *Can you not minister to a mind diseased?*
> *Pluck from the memory a rooted sorrow,*
> *Raze out the written troubles of the brain,*
> *And with some sweet oblivious antidote*
> *Cleanse the heavy heart of that perilous stuff*
> *which weighs upon the soul?*
> *Sometimes the answer is no,*
> *and it is then that the mind goes into free-fall*
> *and drops into the abyss of despair.*

LOVE: FROM THE DARKNESS TO THE LIGHT

A mustang needs to be a free spirit, not corralled and barred from roaming the prairies of euphoric blissfulness that lay like a shining beacon lighting the way to paradise. If not let roam free, a wild mustang will be stifled, trained for subservience and made to wither and grovel before its master, rather than soaring to the heights of glory reserved for the wild and free. Aaron's mind was racing now as he looked into her eyes and could see the pain on her face. Jasmine must still love him, he thought. Yes, she had left him, but there was still love there. She had found him hadn't she? Yes, in the end, she came to him, came to him in all his despair so that he could breathe his last breath in her presence.

THE MONSTER WITHIN

The head sometimes rules the heart.
It becomes its partner in crime.
And the person who commits the crime
Buries it in the deep recesses of the psyche,
Letting it rest there without disturbance,
Should cause you great chagrin
But you are unaware of the monster within.

MESSENGER OF LOVE

My love for you now only knows humility.
I steal into the alleys of darkness that surround me,
Longing to kiss one lock of your hair.
I cannot free myself, because I am your prisoner,
And I cannot break the chains that bind me.

I cannot love myself more than I love you.
I have died and can only be resurrected by you.
I have vanished from the horizon of hope without you.
I have sacrificed all my learning at the alter of faith for you.

LOVE: FROM THE DARKNESS TO THE LIGHT

Alas, I can only be a scholar by knowing love from you.
I have lost all my strength in a torrent of passion.
The power to enable me – yes, can only from you.

I am your knight in shining armour.
Come by my side and I will open the gate to paradise.
Come settle with me, and we shall be
neighbours with the stars.
You have been hiding for so long, drifting endlessly in
Stormy seas where the beacon
of my love could not reach you.
Still, you are connected to me as sure
as the fetus is connected
To the mother by the umbilical cord of life.

Concealed, revealed into the unknown,
in the un-manifested
You must reach out to embrace that which is within me.
You have been a wanderer in the wildness of love lost.
For you, I will be the roaring ocean
pounding the shore of hope.
Come merge with me and leave the world of doubt,
Ignorance and turmoil behind
as we move toward the light of promise.
Be with me! Be with me! Be with me! Please be with me!
I will open the gate to promise and security.
I desire you more than I long
for the nourishment of food or drink.
I thirst and hunger like a lost soul
for one nod of hope from you.
My body, my senses, my mind long for your taste.
I can sense your over-powering presence in my heart.
Even if you are with another,
thinking it is rapturous contentment.
I wait with silent passion for one gesture,
one glance from you.

LOVE: FROM THE DARKNESS TO THE LIGHT

As I cry tears waiting for your acknowledgement,
I realize they are sacred raindrops from the heart.
They are not a mark of weakness, but of power.
They speak the words I cannot muster.
They speak more eloquently than 100,000 tongues.
The tears are messengers of my love.

WHAT ELSE CAN I SAY

Each night I lie in bed thinking of what I had.
Oh, the thought you are gone makes me so sad.
I treasured you and never treated you like a possession,
And I never exercised any aggression.
If only you had known that you were treasured,
And that every step I took was precisely measured.
I should have had more sense than to push you away.
But I made colossal miscalculations every day.
Too often I spoke in haste but never with anger.
Still, somehow I placed your fragile heart in danger.
I never realized that you had corralled your love,
And were just waiting for me to make the final shove.
My inner turmoil boiled with frustration,
But for you I still had great admiration.
Oh, how I wish I could kiss you again with care.
You are my life, my hope, my promise dear.
I loved and treasured each day.

CAN I HAVE HER ON THE OTHER SIDE

She says I should move on,
but she doesn't understand my pain.
I just want her in my arms again.
She loves another now.
I wish I could forget her,
but just don't know how.

LOVE: FROM THE DARKNESS TO THE LIGHT

I lie forlorn every day singing her song,
Knowing with him she is laughing while I am alone.
I wish I believed in God so I could pray.
Maybe it would help me get through the day.
Loving her forever can't be wrong.
How I wish she wasn't gone.

There is no remedy
as the pain goes on.
Her face burned into my mind
playing the pasts sweet melody.
Here soul is haunting me.
I am blind and cannot see.

Every time I close my eyes I see her,
and the dream she decided to defer.
No one compares to her.
What will I do in eternity
but wait for her to arrive.
Can I have her on the other side?

Who wants to be strong
when your true love is gone?
I wait for her return.
Ah, why can't I learn.
Her soul haunts me.
If only my pain she would see.

She was my paradise.
No one compares to her.
I try to look for a paramour.
But her memory closes the door.
Sometimes I wish for the final night.
It would obliterate her from my sight.

There is no relief.

LOVE: FROM THE DARKNESS TO THE LIGHT

I see her in my sleep.
Others are rushing me,
But I can still see her touching me.
I wallow in darkness dreaming of her,
Waiting for the final curtain to occur.

Damn, damn, damn where is she now?
Every time I close my eyes it is hope lost.
Why, why must I pay this abominable cost.
What will I do in eternity
but wait for her to arrive.
Can I have her on the other side?

EMPTY TO THE CORE

Why am I such a fool?
I can't stop myself from loving you.
And countless nights I've cried for you,
Just because my feelings are true.
I walk around a mansion up and down;
Your things are all around.
I long for you to come back to me.
I am so blind and cannot see.

I've spent so long waiting for you.
No, there's nothing I can do.
I can't stop myself from loving you,
Even though I want to.
I can cry all I want,
But I can't pass it off as nonchalant.
My feelings can't just fly away.
They are here to stay.

I tried to cast you aside for awhile.
But no other one could beguile.
I wrapped myself in the arms of another,

LOVE: FROM THE DARKNESS TO THE LIGHT

While you moved away from me further and further.
The pain just want recede.
It is you I need.
You find me abhorrent I know.
But I just can't let you go.

You will never know how much I cry,
While alone I forlornly lie.
I want to move on and have a life.
But, I just can't lick this strife.
I sit by anxiously awaiting a call.
But the silence just makes me ball.
Heartache makes my insides sore.
Without you, I am empty to the core.

THE COST OF LOVE

When you have cried a river of tears,
When you have given your all,
When you have apologized and pleaded,
When you have battled sadness and depression,
Then, you know the cost of love.

When love dictates you want her contented.
When you worry about her choices in lovers.
When you hurt inside to protect her.
When you know she is forever gone.
Then, you know the cost of love.

When you fight to keep her safe.
When you know she is all alone.
When you struggle to help her.
When you sigh with hope.
Then, you know the cost of love.

When you look for another.

LOVE: FROM THE DARKNESS TO THE LIGHT

When you still care.
When you still seek her favour.
When you still want her happy.
Then, you know the cost of love.

When she smiles with appreciation.
When she values your counsel.
When she reaches out with warmth.
When she wants to be your friend.
Then, you know the cost was worth it.

THE FAITHFUL HEART

He stood on the burning deck of desire.
Whence it appeared his lover had fled;
The flame that lit his heart was a flickering fire. Floating
like a vapour all about his head.
Yet bold and bright he stood.
As born to rule the love storm;
True love coursing through his blood
He sought her in magnificent form.
The flames rolled on, but he would not go
Without her soft word;
He could sense death below,
Her voice no longer heard.
With hope, faith and affection fair,
That well had borne their part
The noblest thing which perished there
Was that dependent faithful heart.

I WILL LOVE YOU UNTIL THE DAY I DIE

How do you stop loving someone to the core
who simply does not love you anymore?
Countless nights and days I cry for you,
because my feelings are so true.

LOVE: FROM THE DARKNESS TO THE LIGHT

I have patiently waited for your return.
Oh, for you I forlornly yearn.
I simply can't stop missing you,
no matter what I do.

You can treat me like dirt,
and with others endlessly flirt.
I want to move on with my life,
but inside me there is still strife.

Inside you there is bottled up hate,
which makes me know it is too late.
All I can say is I would like to be free.
My transgression I would like to see.

How do you stop loving someone to the core
who simply doesn't love you anymore?
The truth is that no matter how hard I try,
I will want to know what I did until the day I die.

A FOND WISH

You never said you were leaving.
There was not even a goodbye.
You were here one day and gone the next
Without even telling me why.

How I have needed you
And how I have cried.
I loved you dearly and I love you still
As in my heart a emptiness
That nobody else will ever fill.

It broke my heart to lose you,
But you did not go alone,
Because part of me went with you.

LOVE: FROM THE DARKNESS TO THE LIGHT

Oh, how I wish you would come home.

Trust is paramount in any relationship, and when trust is lost, especially when it comes to fidelity, hope of reconciliation is a casualty of the heart, because fear of the repetition of infidelity always plays upon the mind of the aggrieved party, making it difficult to lend trust. Sometimes frivolity helps one deal with infidelity.

MY SWEET LITTLE WHORE

She was once my wife.
In her I did delight.
She is a great beauty.
Men look at her more than twice.
Her eyes dance and sparkle
And shine with great suffice.

Her smile is glamorous,
With teeth gleaming white.
Her body is hot and smooth.
She can wiggle with delight.
Oh my, between her legs
Men's souls take flight.

She gives sex freely to all.
Those lucky enough to be with her
Feel like they are at a fornication ball.
Now I have nothing to infer.
However, within her all men can bore,
Because she is a sweet little whore!

Acts of betrayal are possible from anyone. None of us is perfect, so regardless of what happens, people who have been together for years should not let acrimony keep them from being magnanimous and still showing they care.

LOVE: FROM THE DARKNESS TO THE LIGHT

WATCHING OVER YOU
by
J. Wayne Frye

Love is like steps made of concrete,
Leading to darkness or light.
It can feel cold or warm on your feet.
It can lead to sorrow or shining light.

Light a candle, see it glisten and glow,
17 years we have been through high & low.
When you think of me, think of the light.
It will always be here day or night.

A candle flickers, forgotten and out of sight,
But within there is still a bit of bright.
Though now there is sorrow and sadness
Where was once hope and gladness.

I may not be very near, but I have not gone,
So when you light a candle and watch it glow,
Know that you will never be alone,
Because my river has a slow steady flow.

What came between us was a shrill singer,
And caused the light to flicker and turn blue.
Yet, commitment from me will not linger.
I shall always fondly be watching over you.

LOVE: FROM THE DARKNESS TO THE LIGHT

PART 2
IN PURSUIT OF AN IDEAL THAT PROCLAIMS LOVE CAN BE LOST – AND LOVE CAN BE FOUND

Life is a circuitous road, not a straight thoroughfare.
We shall not cease from the search for truth.
Yet, the end of all our searching will be to
arrive where we started the search
and know the place for the first time.
After the end is before the end.

You may ask what the above means. Put simply, it is saying that life is not a straight road, it is filled with curves, circles, bumps and hills that we think are impediments to progress. However, many things seem preordained. Life is a search for truth - the truth of hope, promise and, above all, love. Yet, when we do all this searching, we wind up eventually at the beginning - back where we started. However, it is as if we will know the place for the first time, because all the curves, circles, bumps and hills will be forgotten after the end of our search. Why? Because we will know love as if it had always been there, and all the searching led us to that which existed in our heart when we began the search. So, wait anxiously for the search to come full circle and to be at the beginning after the end. Confusing? Perhaps, but, then again, love itself is often confusing.

Through the darkness of lost hope, I meandered through corridors of misery thinking that the darkness that engulfed me was so overwhelming that there would be no light to ever brighten the path to redemption. However, my dear friend Bruce Beardsley refused to let me smoulder in hopelessness and forced me to arise from the ashes of despair. It was he who said, "Check out the possibilities Wayne. I found love after 20 years alone. You can also."

LOVE: FROM THE DARKNESS TO THE LIGHT

Into my life in the blinking of an eye came Lynton Viñas. Sometimes all the stars seem to be aligned in perfect harmony. We were both on the verge of giving up on ever finding that special person to make our lives seem complete, when a one in a million opportunity presented itself one night in the nightclub of euphoric merriment, and modern technology let us explore that one in a million connection that had reared its glorious head and brought two searchers in the desert of lost hope into the oasis of bubbling brooks of possibilities.

I am not a believer in fate, but it does seem like there was some mysterious force at play leading to the inevitability of our meeting. She had been looking for four years after a traumatic break up fostered by a boyfriend she found in bed with another woman. For me, it was a six month battle with depression over a wife who had merrily skipped off with a younger man. So, we had both endured heartache, and in each other we almost immediately sensed that the heartache was about to come to an end.

I had great difficulty initially because of out age difference, but for her, in youthful exuberance, she uttered, "Age is just a number. I could get run over by a car any day as I cross the street, and you may live to be 100."

What follows is the poetry and prose of love that was almost instantaneous for both of us. So, although one love was lost for me, another one was found. As one door was closed another door was opened.

A journey of the heart has its ups and downs, but without the search for hope that requires a drive toward what you anticipate will be nirvana, life serves no purpose. So, just when you think all hope is lost and you are about to go over that cliff and fall into the deep abyss of hopelessness, the

LOVE: FROM THE DARKNESS TO THE LIGHT

miracle of lobe rescues you. So, climb in and let's ride down that golden road toward the euphoria of love.

MY MUSE

She is dark-skinned with a radiant glow.
She has deep set alluring brown eyes.
She has a mischievous smile that lights up a room.
She is filled with vitality and restless energy.
She is the purity of the morning dew.
She is the warmth of the noonday sun.
She is the bright full moon at night.
She is the peaceful rain that falls on a warm day.
She is the cool breeze that tempers the heat of despair.
She is my Goddess sent from afar to inspire my soul.
She is the one who brings light to my darkness.
She quinces my hunger and my thirst with love.
She, my fair one is sent from heaven above.

ANGEL OF MY HEART

Oh, how I wish I could be talking to my angel.
She is the angel who restored my lost soul.
She is the angel who mended my broken heart.
She is the angel who shined a light in my darkness.
She is the angel who gave me hope.
She is the angel my heart will not let go

IN MY WARM ARMS

I anxiously await the day when we will meet.
It will be the day God sits at his great judgment seat.
And he will wave his hand in the sky,
as in each others arms we lie.

I am like a kid waiting to get some ice cream,

LOVE: FROM THE DARKNESS TO THE LIGHT

anxiously desiring you, my golden dream.
Together things will work out fine.
Our intertwined lives will be divine.
It does not matter how long I must wait,
because being together is our fate.
As days tick by with the thread of time.
I long for the perfect hour when you are mine.

You are the face I see when I close my eyes.
And in the morning I see you again as time flies.
You are my fantasy and my reality of hope.
Without having you with me, I could not cope.

So wait patiently in your golden lair my love.
The day will come when I fly to you like a dove.
Do not despair and raise any desperate alarms,
For soon, I shall wrap you in my warm arms.

MY HOPE

My heart feels soft and tender with hope.
It is a crackling ember, a soft flame of hope.
Every time I gaze upon you it shines a light of hope.
In the end, I realize you, and only you, are my hope.

True love – sought by all – found by few.

DON'T WAKE ME

I dream of being with you.
I dream of your soft touch.
I do not want to awaken
Because you are here only in my dreams.

Let me sleep and close my eyes.

LOVE: FROM THE DARKNESS TO THE LIGHT

For then, I am with you.
I feel you.
I hear you.
My dreams bring us together.
Before you, I had no life.
I didn't think a woman like you could exist.
Oh, let me sleep, so I am with you.

I dream you are with me.
I dream you touch me.
I dream you kiss me.
I dream you fondle me.

Let me sleep.
For in sleep I am with you.
I float in sweet bliss.
Don't wake me please.

I float on a cloud of your soft caress.
I meander in a field of clover with you.
I breathe the air of love in my sleep.
Don't wake me. Don't wake me.

WHERE YOU ARE MEANT TO BE

On a web cam I can see your smile.
Oh, how I want to touch your face.
You bring me such joy with your love
That is as soft and fine as Belgium lace.

We cannot touch, but I still feel you.
Your laughter is music to my ears.
Your voice whispers a melody of affection
And wipes away all my lonely tears.

I imagine you here by my side.

LOVE: FROM THE DARKNESS TO THE LIGHT

I will hold you warmly next to me.
This, my lovely home on the hill
Is where you are meant to be.

HEAVEN FOUND

Your sweetness is only exceeded by your beauty.
I hope when you set eyes on me
and I wrap you in my arms for the first time
you will not be disappointed,
because to disappoint you
would be to fail as a human being.
I expect nothing from you physically
but a glow in your eyes
that reflects that you know you
have a man who adores you
and bows before your altar of love
to humbly beseech you to allow me your favour.
I am too old to be robustly virile.
I am too physically displeasing to be an Adonis.
The middle age spread is a constant battle
that I lose more often than win.
My hair, what there is of it,
is greying more each day.
I now have aches and pains
that were never there before.
The clock of time beats inexorably forward,
but it now is held in abeyance
by a thirst to never leave you,
because when the grim reaper's call is heard
I shall tell him to scurry off,
because I have already found heaven on earth.

Love is an echo of the heart.

LOVE: FROM THE DARKNESS TO THE LIGHT

KNOWING YOU: ESSAY OF LOVE

I laid down on my sofa blissfully reflecting on all the wonderful times I have shared with you. Each day is spent in joyous thoughts of you, and how I want to spend the rest of my life in heavenly bliss with you by my side as I float on a cloud of love sailing high above all strife and pain, because with you there is only euphoric elation. You are the ripe nectar in the flower of love that spreads out its welcoming blossoms to greet each day. With you, I have everything in life I desire. Without you, I would be in a barren desert of misery dying of thirst for your love. You quench my thirst for affection as I see your love for me spread out its warm arms and embrace me. You are the blood of love that pumps through my veins, making it possible for me to live. My heart beats with a steady rhythm of adoration for she who has become my whole world.

You can talk with someone for years but never really know them. I talked to you for 10 minutes and saw deep inside you a compassionate heart that longed to be embraced by he who would make your life complete. I knew the depth of your character instantly. Connections are made with the heart, not the tongue. I still am mystified that I am the lucky one to win your heart.

I can sit and look at you without saying a word to you or hearing a word from you, but I can still hear you in my heart. I feel like I am a newborn baby, because before I met you I was not alive. I now have you with me 24 hours a day as you are in a picture frame looking over my shoulder.

You are the calm that quiets my worry, and you are the last chapter in my book of love. My darling I am yours from now until forever. Rest peacefully tonight in the

LOVE: FROM THE DARKNESS TO THE LIGHT

assurance that you have found your champion of love. Only death can keep from you, and even the grim reaper will find me a worthy opponent as I will fight to never leave your side even when death calls, because heaven would not be heaven without you.

HARMONIOUS HAPPINESS

I talk to you when I should be writing. I long for you when I should be writing. I pine for you when I should be writing. I look at your pictures when I should be writing. I close my eyes and imagine your mischievous smile when I should be writing. I daydream of your dark dancing eyes when I should be writing. I long to hear your soft melodic voice when I should be writing. I lament not being able to look upon your angelic face when I should be writing. Still, you are my muse and motivate me to let words flow from my heart onto paper - words that are motivated by you and your loveliness of mind, body and soul. Thank you my sweet Lynton. Ah, the name is so melodious. It rolls off my lips like water gently bubbling over rocks in a slow moving stream. The word Lynton plays like a symphony of harmonious contentment in my mind. Lynton, Lynton, Lynton, Lynton……………………………………………..

ENDURING LOVE

When the shades of night come I cannot sleep.
Why? Because my love for you runs so deep.
You, to me, are a reflection in a golden eye.
Beside your warm body I long to lie.

You feel my love from afar.
Distance our love cannot mar.
I long to touch your soft skin
And feel your soul deep within.

LOVE: FROM THE DARKNESS TO THE LIGHT

Oh, when I cannot see that which I miss,
I dream of a long, tender, lingering kiss.
Your lips are like ripe grapes from the vine.
I am blessed to know you are mine.

Knowing that distance keeps us apart
Stills the rhythm of my pounding heart.
You are the a phantom of my mind,
Because you are so loving and kind.

Each night when we conclude our skype.
My mind is filled with a guiding light.
I must write to you my sweetheart so pure,
And let you know that for all-time my love will endure

THE GREATEST TREASURE

Sitting alone where there used to be companionship leads one to contemplate mortality and reflect upon that which brought joy. In my life, there are things that burn brightly in my heart as I await that which beckons us all. I had a grandmother who loved me deeply and was always trying to assuage my lonely childhood misery caused by anguish dealing with a father who did not know how to love. Then there was Jasmine who came along and for 20 years made me feel genuinely alive. Of course, I embrace in the deepest regions of reflection the childhood that I shared with my children. I had no childhood of my own, so they finally gave me one vicariously as a young adult. Now, I have you to treasure Lynton until the siren call of eternity. I have your love and that is the greatest treasure I have ever possessed.

> **Love is like a rose – it's beautiful but has thorns that can tear your flesh and cause pain.**

LOVE: FROM THE DARKNESS TO THE LIGHT

Days float blissfully by now like a fluffy cloud high in the sky. My life has been reduced to waiting. Yes, waiting for those two phone calls each day from my love that is far away in distance, but oh so close in my heart. How, I ask myself each day, can an old man receive love so dear from her who quickens my pulse and makes my heart beat with the rhythm of attachment, devotion, ardour and frenzied excitement? You are a golden tear I shed each day in contemplative reflection of a life now filled with the gracious unselfish kindness of she who brings a twinkle to my eye, she who reaches into the depths of my soul to shine a beacon of light into the darkness, she who kisses my loneliness away with moist, wet, succulent lips of passion. I gaze upon that angelic face and can see your affection floating like a vapour in the humid summer air as it lifts me from the cold and warms me. I want to amorously devour not just your body, but your soul. I want to worship at your altar of love, embracing your kindness, courtesy, unselfishness and benevolent tenderness. You are the raging fire that sears my soul and burns away despair. Oh, how I love you.

LOVE'S GREAT LIGHT

Outside my window I hear the gentle breeze,
As it caress the leaves from the tall trees,
And carries them flittering all around,
Then they gently fall upon the ground.

I see the birds so high above,
Their songs chirping of love.
And laid upon their soft sweet wing
My affection for you they bring.

And as they start their graceful descent,
Delivering a message that's serenely sent,

LOVE: FROM THE DARKNESS TO THE LIGHT

I want you to know to me you are so dear
And I forlornly wish you were near.

Upon your soft breast I would lay my weary head,
Letting my affection upon you spread.
A day has never passed without thoughts of you.
Ah, how many times did I miss your cue?
The ravages of time can shake me to the core,
But one golden moment with you makes my spirits soar.
I can now do that which I wanted for so long,
But circumstances prevented me from singing the song.

Is it never too late
To finally welcome fate?
True devotion and affection I cannot fight.
For you have shined upon me love's great light

Love is fuel for the heart.

AFFECTION IS A GREAT GIFT

My affection keeps growing
Like the flowers in the spring.
And when they are fully opened
They are such a beautiful thing.

My affection keeps growing
Between your heart and mine,
Always staying connected
By the past's invisible twine.

My affection keeps growing
Like the twinkling stars in the sky.
You can never hide from me,
As tears of love form in my eyes.

LOVE: FROM THE DARKNESS TO THE LIGHT

My affection keeps growing
Like the chirping of a singing bird.
I know that my heart pounds
With your every spoken word.

My affection keeps growing,
And it gives me a soaring lift.
I sincerely hope you know
That love is my finest gift.

Love is the elixir of life.

SYMPTOMS OF LOVE

The symptoms of a disease will last 1 or 2 days,
but the fever of my love will last forever.

NEVER IGNORE YOUR VALUE

Underestimating your worth
allows others to ignore your value.
Never fall for anyone
who is not willing to catch you.

You are with me day and night in my mind.
I look at those succulently soft thick soft lips
and dream of tasting your sweetness
as they are pressed against mine.

I long to wrap my arms around you and cling to you.
I want to feel your warmth next to me,
and have my arms around that
which gives me the sustenance of love.
My priority has become you in all that I do.
You are what sustains me.

LOVE: FROM THE DARKNESS TO THE LIGHT

Knowing I am loved by you
Brightens the darkness that often surrounds me.

I know you have endured poverty.
I know you have endured abuse.
I know you have endured injustice,
Ridicule, disharmony and disdain.

But never underestimate your worth
because that allows others to ignore your value.
And never again fall for anyone
who is not willing to catch you.
I am here my sweet to catch you –
no, I have caught you!

SO MUCH

If I die tomorrow
tell it to the trees
how much I loved you.
Tell it to the soft breeze
that rustles leaves to the ground
that you are my world.
Tell it to the sky above
that I adore you.

Tell it to soft summer rain,
even it would understand.
Tell it to your dog,
whose bark reminds you
of how much you are loved by me.
Tell it to a wall made of stone,
shout it in the city streets
how much I love you.
But don't shout it too loud,
because people will not believe you.

LOVE: FROM THE DARKNESS TO THE LIGHT

No one could comprehend,
no one could possibly believe
that you are loved so much.
They simply could not understand
how one man could love one woman
so much, so much, so much.

THE MISUNDERSTANDING

She thought I neglected her.
She cried.
I thought she neglected me.
I cried.
We both thought it was goodbye.
We cried.
But the truth is we are connected forever.
So, there is never any need to cry.

MY WARM LOVING ARMS

Distance between us cannot separate,
Nor former agony in our hearts discriminate.
The distance cannot keep us apart,
Because we carry each other in our hearts.
Before we had good times and bad.
We were often happy but also sad.
We were about to give up our quest.
But now we share a love-fest.
You love me and I believe it's true.
My darling I love you too.
You amaze and delight me in every way.
Your vamping takes my breath away.
I will wrap you in my arms and hold tight.
I will never let you out of my sight.
Each day I love you more and more.
I absolutely never felt like this before.

LOVE: FROM THE DARKNESS TO THE LIGHT

I want to blow whistles, bells, sirens and alarms;
And hold you in my warm loving arms.

YOU ARE THE ONLY ONE

I love only you.
You are my world now.
Everything I do each day
Is directed toward making your life perfect.
I want to build you a love cottage,
Where we will bask in glorious affection.
You often voice fear that I might leave,
But never fret or be jealous,
Because you are my life now.
Do not think that I would want
Any life without you in it.
Without you, I have no life.

Since meeting you, life has a different meaning.
I dream of kissing those soft, succulent, luscious, thick lips.
One look into your longing dark eyes sends me
On a voyage into a sea of tranquility.
Your incredible smile brings untold joy,
And your laughter lifts my spirits.

You are the best thing that ever happened in my life.
Never be jealous of anyone, because no one
Can take your place in my heart.
It is I, who should have the jealousy,
Because men are not only attracted by your looks,
But by your inner beauty that shines brilliantly.

You are a beacon of promise, hope and love.
You are the sunshine of my life.
Never doubt my affection darling.
I am devoted to you.

LOVE: FROM THE DARKNESS TO THE LIGHT

And I shall devote my life
Trying to be worthy of your love.

Part of learning to love someone is getting acquainted with their friends, and seeing the joy in the things the one you love does, even if it can sometimes seem a bit silly. The following poem was the first poem I wrote about my muse Lynton and her dear friend Ingrid. As I often tell people, Lynton's two best friends, Ingrid and Channa make getting Lynton a package deal, because all three of them are such special women and are so devoted to on another.

INGRID AND LYNTON'S HANGOVER SUNDAY

Crawled in at 6:00 AM almost dead.
They woke up on Sunday.
Oh, how hard to get out of bed.
They both had a very sore head.

Just thinking about the fun.
Oh, what had they done?
Faded eyeliner and lipstick gone.
They checked to see if they were alone.

The men had eyed them in the drinker's lair.
These were two girls as hot as fire.
Legs like fine woven soft silk.
They were all honey dew and milk.

Lynton looks at Ingrid and shakes her head.
Headaches pound because frivolity they fed.
Think they would do this foolish thing again.
Of course they would, nothing wrong with a little sin.

> Love is the soft sounds of blissfulness in the heart
> that plays the sweet symphony of affection.

LOVE: FROM THE DARKNESS TO THE LIGHT

A JOURNEY OF THE HEART

Come on, take the long journey
on the ship of love that will let you
fly to me across the sea.
It is getting you closer to me.
It is not just a passport.
It is a ticket to my arms.

Fly with the wings of my love for you.
Feel with the wisdom of my affection.
Bury all sorrow, make a place for the new.
Rejoice in what will come and be daring.
And don't let anything frighten you.
Make the journey of the heart to me

LOVE'S ETERNAL LIGHT
IN THE EMBRACE OF HOPE

I anxiously awaited your call, but there is only silence.
Without hearing your voice,
part of me is missing - the best part.
You are like a phantom in the night,
preying precipitously upon my mind.
If I cannot see you, hear you, feel your presence
there is a hole in my heart.

There is a little game that I joyously like to play.
Where I close my eyes and gently fade away.
I transport myself to a special place
Beyond the moon, the stars and space.

In this special place all I can see
Is you my dear and of course me.
Together we fondly embrace so tight
As we find love's eternal light.

J. WAYNE FRYE

LOVE: FROM THE DARKNESS TO THE LIGHT

E-MAIL PROCLAIMING OUR HEARTS ARE ONE

You are sleeping now as it is late night where you abide, but I am e-mailing you simply because it makes me feel closer to you, almost as if I was there lovingly by your side, looking at you in the dark, watching your chest rise up and down rhythmically as you breathe. Looking at you in sweet repose, I would long to kiss your thick succulent lips and to stroke your alluringly soft body, but would not because it would awaken you. You are so precious and fragile like a fine piece of china. I would probably get a tear in my eye as I gazed upon you and thought to myself how lucky I am to have the love of such a remarkable woman. I will conclude this e-mail now, but my love for you shall never be concluded, not even after my death. It will live forever in your heart, as you have now made my heart and yours one.

SHE MEETS HER DESTINY

You are about to embark on a great journey of hope.
I long to be with you but alas cannot so I mope.
Yet, my pride in you shall never cease,
Because in my heart upon you I feast.
It is you that I reverentially admire,
As everything you do will inspire.
You are never a quitter I can see,
Your positivism brings joy to me.
You are a woman who is truly rare,
So many talents, with the world you share.
Just the way you make others feel,
Is so magnificent it is almost unreal.
Wherever you go, whatever you seek,
I know you will climb the highest peak.
Each day as to hope you drive,
Know that I am here to help you thrive.

LOVE: FROM THE DARKNESS TO THE LIGHT

MY LOVE SLEEPS

My love sleeps.
Her heart and soul are at peace,
knowing she is loved by me.
She is more beautiful than
any work of art every produced,
because no painting by any artist,
no stroke of the brush
can adequately capture such beauty.

Silence fills the walls of my room,
and the day is calm,
as my thoughts are like the trees
taking deep root into the earth of my soul.
Towering mountains and the stars
that shine above them
rise into an endless
tribute to she who sleeps.

I wonder in her dreams
what places she sees,
the weather and colours,
the faces and events.
I am moved
by her quiet beauty
that dwells in my heart.
Ah, my love sleeps.

SWEET BLISS

The first time I looked at you my heart skipped a beat.
I knew right away that we had been destined to meet.
I breathed heavily and my stomach was in a knot so tight.
Oh, but in my heart I knew everything was just right.

LOVE: FROM THE DARKNESS TO THE LIGHT

I was timid but felt euphoric when you spoke to me.
Just looking at you brought me great glee.
I was immediately in love with you that day.
My loneliness you completely swept away.

I have never loved anyone so much before.
Of you, I want more and more.
Every word I utter to you is sincere,
Because I love you so much my dear.

You are the world to me and now we are one.
There will be years of great mirth and fun.
I want to be with you the rest of my life.
With you there will be an end to all strife.

There are happy days around the corner now.
We will be together somewhere, somehow.
Being with you is what matters most my dear.
In our lives now we need not have any fear.

When I sweep you in my arms very soon,
I will no doubt purr and swoon.
I long for those succulent lips to give me a kiss.
Then off together we will go and enjoy sweet bliss.

ECHOES OF LOVE FROM AFAR

It is only a short time now since I left my dear love in a far off land. How I long for her as I as I sorrowfully walk about my palatial estate recalling the blissfulness of the time I spent with her in harmonious contentment in a fairy tale land where we shared happiness, hope and love. I only hear echoes of memories of the time with her as if they are embedded in stone. Though I shall soon be in her arms again, I still fondly embrace here alone the echoes of our love.

LOVE: FROM THE DARKNESS TO THE LIGHT

My world revolves around this woman who captured my heart and soul. With her, I am always busy with a life that filled with love, affection and happiness. Today, I live in a house vibrating with echoes of she whom I left behind, but I am still filled with glorious glee, as I embrace the gloriousness of my new life with her where all is possible because of my devotion to her and willingness to throw caution to the wind to support her in all her endeavours and embrace the magnificence of hope and promise she displays.

The thump, thump, thump of her bare feet on the tile floor in our Philippines love nest echoes in my mind day and night. The echoes of her euphonious laughter, captivating smile and singing talents fill the emptiness I endure without her.

I open the blinds on windows to let in some sun and a see shadows play on the stairs and think of her dainty feet pounding about in our little home near the babbling creek where she is always flashing that captivating, mischievous smile as she scurries about.

Happiness abounds in my furtive mind, though we are forlornly apart. I hear the sounds of echoes, echoes of a soft, melodic voice that lights the darkness. I hear sounds of merriment with friends, boisterous laughter, and the melodious music from the sweet voice of euphoric glory. I can hear her sensuous giggle that brings a tingle to my libido. I can hear the murmuring of those magnificent words "I love you" as she and I drifted off to sleep in each others arms.

Our little home is filled with the quiet, but noisy the sounds of love. I glide through this big lonely house now, only hearing echoes, the echoes of glorious love. Oh, how I

LOVE: FROM THE DARKNESS TO THE LIGHT

long to feel her warmth, to embrace her and hold her tight.
Listen to the echoes. Listen to the echoes.

ABIDING LOVE

When the night has come
and the land is covered in darkness,
when the moon is the only light there is,
look at its brightness in the heavens
and you can sense the glowing intensity
of my deep abiding love for you.

IN YOUR ARMS AT LAST

I will miss you at night as I gaze upon the stars.
I will miss you during the day as clouds cover my sun.
I will miss you and want to hold you in my arms.
I will miss you so much, my dear, as each day is done.
I will miss your smile, your joy, your Angie lips.
I will wish you were here, as my loneliness grips.
My mind will travel to far places seeking your beauty..
My heart will beat faster and faster with your memory.
My soul fading that which brings joy, my eyes all teary.
My days will go by so slowly, oh so slowly.
This painful of longing penetrates my heart deeply.
My soul cries out for you more and more strongly.
You are my dear love, my life, my everything.
I yearn for the day we will be together for evermore.
For that day my soul cries out in anguished pursuit.
I reach toward the heavens my love to implore.
Each day away will tediously go by like
sand slowly dripping through an hourglass,
Until I will be in your arms at last.

> Where love dwells, darkness is stayed by destiny's light.

LOVE: FROM THE DARKNESS TO THE LIGHT

THREE WOMEN - SENSUAL AND UNTAMED

The beauty of these three women
Is not in the clothes they wear,
The figure that they carry,
Or the way they comb their hair.

The beauty of these three woman
Can be reflected from their eyes,
Because that is the doorway to their hearts,
The place where true beauty resides.

The beauty of these three women
Grows like a diamond from coal,
The true beauty in these women
Is reflected in the depth of their soul.

It is the caring they lovingly give,
The passion that they divinely show.
The beauty of these three women,
with passing years will grow and grow.

They harken of soft caresses and kisses.
And what is in a name that kindles a flame?
The names are a melody on the winds of time.
Lynton, Channa, Ingrid-wild allure-sensual and untamed.

BEAUTY IS IN THEIR NAMES

I dreamed I stood looking down from a hill.
At my feet were things of gold I deemed.
With buds and blossoms flowering at will
There were three wonders of which I dreamed.

Among the swaying white lilies in the field,
Walked three comely, vivacious young women,

LOVE: FROM THE DARKNESS TO THE LIGHT

And many a man's heart had they sealed.
Oh, so divinely beautiful my sanity was trimming.

Dark eyes of allure blinked in the noonday sun,
As Ingrid, Channa and Lynton blessed the valley below
Causing men to wantonly fantasize about fun,
As love was the seed they wanted to wantonly sow.

These three had been exquisitely nurtured by the stars.
As they were like the waving lilies I had seen.
Oh, for all God's Glory no nightfall mars
The luminous beauty of these three who gleam.

Sensual lips slowly and provocatively unfurl,
And men long for the softness of the mouth.
Ah, how one would want to lay the crimson world,
And gasp in delight at the glories these three count.

They are three golden dreams that make you want to fill
Your cup of love and delight to the brim
And shout with glee of the soaring flames
That break down your heart, palpitates your pulse,
Quickens your breath and destroys your will.
Lynton, Channa and Ingrid – Lynton, Channa and Ingrid
glorious beauty is in their names.

THE HEART IS A LONELY HUNTER

How wonderful it is to realize
You are deeply loved by someone?
It is that one moment; that one instance,
When it crystallizes in your mind?
All the "I love you's" suddenly become more meaningful,
Much more than just mere words.
Genuine love is something that is not heard.
It is felt deep within one's soul.

LOVE: FROM THE DARKNESS TO THE LIGHT

A few tears, a look of consternation
when you part says more than words.
Watching the reaction of a person
Who in melancholy sheds tears?
When knowing you will be apart
Makes you realize that the heart is a lonely hunter.
Love is often incredibly painful,
Because it is an emotion of the heart.
Tonight I saw that love from
She whom I lovingly adore.
My words had touched her before,
But it was not my words tonight.
She cried because she loved me
So much and did not want me to leave.
Yes, tonight my angel cried tears from heaven.
Those tears rained down into my heart,
Soaking, no, saturating it with love.
I saw the love she had for me,
And now realize my obligation.
Yes, the heart is indeed a lonely hunter,
But tonight the hunter is stayed.
As Houseman once said,
Home is the sailor, home from sea
That he loves so dearly.
Home is the hunter from the hill,
Fast in the boundless snare
All flesh lies taken at his will
And every fowl of air.
'Tis evening and I am free,
And in the distance of the heart
It is hope I can see.
The starlit wave is still:
Home is the sailor from the sea,
And the hunter from the hill.
Ah, I have been pierced with the arrow of love,
And no longer is the heart a lonely hunter.

LOVE: FROM THE DARKNESS TO THE LIGHT

THE FLAME OF LOVE

Within my heart a candle burns
and somehow you seem to know
my spirit is captured in the flame
and it won't allow me to let you go.
And in the window of your heart
shines a bright candlelight;
placed there to greet me la while ago
from the shadows of the night.
In times of peril, you find me.
A candle draws us near.
As our love glows in the darkness,
its beauty calms the fear.

A candle burns deep inside
with a light all its own.
When you become aware of it
you know you are not alone.
A candle glows within your heart
lit by me a while ago,
where I can be remembered
when your spirits might be low.
A candle's flame can sometimes flicker,
even appear to almost go out.
But its light can roar to life
bringing brightness all about.
Today I felt your presence with
The flame a glistening shine
as it glowed brightly,
showing you are kind.

My best wishes embrace you,
with the light of eternal hope my dear,
because now you are here deep within,
and it means neither of us has to fear.

LOVE: FROM THE DARKNESS TO THE LIGHT

TO MY LOVE AT CHRISTMAS

It was Christmas and I would celebrate it alone this year.
Yet, it was not a season without cheer.
It was almost as if I was fighting a lover's war.
This holiday was different from those before.

I had no packages under the tree wrapped with care.
Yet, a pretty woman had taken away despair.
I have forgotten Christmas of the past.
This was the Christmas with memories to last.

Her photo decks a spot in on my desk of pine.
It offers a new love at this most special time.
I will pick it up and hold it close to my heart,
Promising her devotion and that we will never part.

I have to abide the clarion call.
I pledge to give her my all.
I shall never leave her behind,
Because she is my special find.

In loneliness I will reach up,
And savour from my lover's cup.
I shall reach out in a loving way,
Knowing that with her, things are OK.

On this most celebrated day,
Physically she is far away.
But to her on fleet wings,
My love flies and sings.

I may not have any Christmas lights,
But I can still see wondrous sights.
She is in my heart all night and day.
Ah, I love her. What else can I say?

LOVE: FROM THE DARKNESS TO THE LIGHT

TO MY MUSE ONCE AGAIN FROM DEEP WITHIN

I glanced at you and my heart began to sing.
My thoughts buzzed like a locust in flight.
Your voice belled forth, and the sunlight bent.
Suddenly you were my new way of looking at things.
You allowed me to live again.
Every glance at the world made me
realize you were my salvation.
We are inextricably twinned in the sands of time.
You make me pick up my pen when on the wing
and force me shape new words I didn't expect,
flapping the old excitement I once felt
when lifted off in flights of fresh creation,
before I learned despair and frustration.
You inflate within me great exhilaration.
Without you I have so much to lose.
Who knows what pleasures years ahead we may choose
Ah, you my darling are my muse!

IT SHINES SO BRIGHT

Alone I challenged the darkness
Forlorn and so very much alone,
With a broken heart no one could atone.
Inside, I felt sorrow.
There was a gust of hopelessness.
Evil patterns danced in my head.
Still I held on waiting for the light,
Knowing the truth would lead me home,
Towards happiness and tranquility.
Then there was one who loved me.
Though in a far away land,
She stood by my side.
Now, I see the light.
Oh, it shines so bright!

LOVE: FROM THE DARKNESS TO THE LIGHT

YOU TOUCHED MY SOUL

Never have I seen the sun shine brighter,
Or so many days seem so precious,
My life so complete
And the feeling of my dreams
Being placed into the palms of my hands
As I did when I was with you.
You touched my soul
With your love.

HOPE AND LOVE

As the earth spins into day and night,
the two of us move toward the light
and no longer fear the darkness.
And as the earth sometimes has foul weather,
the soul too has its typhoons of hopelessness.
Hope and love are what binds us together.
Our love is what sustains us.
Something wonderful lies ahead
and, it beckons us with hope.

We push ever forward together.
Love pulls us and sustains us.
Love is everywhere between us.
We were in love even before we met,
because we were searchers for hope.
Love pulls us into heavenly bliss.
Love is radiant comfort deep in our souls.
Love binds us together.
With hope in our hearts and love connecting us,
we need not fear anything that lies ahead.

When all is seemingly hopeless,
when it is the darkest of days,

LOVE: FROM THE DARKNESS TO THE LIGHT

when there is foul weather all about,
there are two forces to sustain us - hope and love.

SILK AND LACE

Distance is my curse now,
Before the misery of separation I bow.
Distance, ah distance – I long for her.
I want to touch her, caress her, make love to her.

Love should not be thought of tritely
Or be crushed by distance finitely.
It's a feeling honoured rightly.
Lovers never should take it lightly.

In loneliness I ponder.
My thoughts wander.
I long for her embrace.
She is like silk and lace

SHE BRINGS THE LIGHT

There are no stars in heaven that bear her name.
Yet, she is one who deserves great fame.
Inside her is purity of soul.
Kindness is her goal.

She has a fiery spirit
That dwells deep within.
She stands against despair,
And forgives every sin.

Her smile can melt the coldest heart,
Her voice quiet a raging sea,
As she shows great compassion,
and brings others much glee.

LOVE: FROM THE DARKNESS TO THE LIGHT

With her, hope can abide,
As euphoria can be found.
She brings light to the darkness, and
Her melodic voice is such a sweet sound.

With her, darkness has no hope.
It has lost its bite.
She blazes like a comet in the sky,
A dear angel of mercy that brings the light.

A VISION OF LOVE INTO ETERNITY

I knew I loved her dearly,
but since leaving her
I realize just how much I adore her,
because there is a deep emptiness in me
without her by my side.
Her radiant smile is like a beacon
that shines in my heart.
It brightens the darkness and diminishes despair,
making pain and sorrow melt
like butter in the noonday sun.
She has more dignity and grace than any woman
I have ever known.
I put her pictures on my desk,
and I sigh with rapturous ecstasy at her beauty.
Her bronze skin seems to glisten with delight
and her hair shines like polished brass.
Oh, and the sparkle that comes from her eyes
that seem to be dancing with delight.
Yet, all that beauty is secondary to the beauty
she has within, a beauty that will not wrinkle with age,
nor ever fade from my mind.
When I take my last breath
I want to be looking into her eyes,
so I can take the vision with me into eternity.

LOVE: FROM THE DARKNESS TO THE LIGHT

LOVE AND AFFECTION

Never chase love and affection.
If it isn't given freely by another person,
it is not worth having.

THE LUCKIEST MAN ALIVE

I have written many articles for Canadian newspapers over the years, and most have been tirades against the unfairness of an economic system based on greed or attacks on politicians who serve themselves more the citizens who elect them. However, today, I am going to write about something that is actually just as important, although it might seem superfluous initially. I hope I can make everyone realize the value of a smile in a world where frowns are the norm.

Almost a year ago, my life came crashing down in turmoil as my wife ran off with another man, leaving me to ask why I should suffer such a fate. Although we have remained friends out of respect and genuine affection for one another, the hurt was so intense that I often felt like I had an anvil placed upon my chest. After many months of misery, I finally accepted the fact that I had to get on with whatever life I had left. It was then that I found a free dating site, and after a few weeks of dealing with women more interested in money than affection, I was about to shrug my shoulders and simply resign myself to spending the rest of my life alone. Then, as a religious person would say, a miracle came along.

This miracle was in the form of a 5:2, 105 pound dynamic Filipino whirl-wind of unbridle energy named Lynton. I knew from the very first e-mail that this was a woman of incredible beauty, but more important, a woman

LOVE: FROM THE DARKNESS TO THE LIGHT

with great depth of character. Unlike the other Filipino women with whom I communicated, she never asked for any money. She didn't even hint at it. This was a woman who had great pride in herself and her independence. Yes, I was mesmerized by her beauty, but more important; I was satiated with respect and admiration for a woman of genuine character. Oh, and the smile, her smile shined like a beacon in the night as it devoured the darkness that surrounded me.

Her smile was free, but was the most valuable commodity I have ever encountered. It enriched my life and gave me hope. It happened the first time I conversed with her on Skype in a flash and it has lasted forever. Now, I cannot get along without that smile. A day without it is like a day without nourishment. It creates happiness and joy in my heart and captivates my soul. It is rest for my weariness, daylight to my darkness, sunshine to my sadness, and nature's best antidote for my troubled heart. Yet it cannot be bought, begged, borrowed, or stolen, for it is something that is no earthly good to anybody until it is given away, and she gives it freely to me. I had no smiles left to give until her smile made my lips expand with glee that someone could actually care so much for me. Today, I am resurrected from the depths of despair, because of a smile that says, "I love you." So, to all of you out there with frowns on your faces, I say that it is time to part those lips, show those teeth and let the world luxuriate in the beauty of your smile. I bask in the exquisiteness of Lynton's smile everyday, and it shines a light that penetrates my soul and makes my spirit soar to the heavens. I am the luckiest man alive.

JOURNEY TO PARADISE

Sometimes my love for you is so overwhelming

LOVE: FROM THE DARKNESS TO THE LIGHT

that when I see you frustrated with the flow of events
in our lives it buries me in despair
to not be able to make things magically
occur the way you want.
All I desire in life is to be with you.
I never dreamed I would love someone this much.
How do you describe a love that is all-consuming
and flows like a raging river through
a towering gorge headed to the sea?
There is only calm in my heart
when I can look into your eyes,
when I can gaze upon that incredible smile
that would melt the heart of a savage,
when I can see that mischievous vamping
manifested in your twinkling eyes and coy manner,
when I can hear that melodic voice
that seems to float on a soft cloud of mirth and joy
as in response to one of my questions you utter,
"of course" with an infliction of intent
that makes my heart palpitate.
Oh, and when I touch you.
How I long to reach out and feel your softness again,
to gently caress your brown skin
that glistens in the soft air of desire.
It is so much more than a sexual attraction.
It is an act that soothes my soul and calms my fears.
To kiss your soft lips is like drinking from the river of hope
in a heaven reserved for only those lucky enough to bask
in the radiant light that glistens from you
like a divine glow from God himself.
You are my God, because I worship you
and bow before your altar of sweetness, kindness and love.
How, I ask myself, can this woman love me?
How can I be the luckiest man in the world
to have her melt in my arms,
sigh with delight as I share

LOVE: FROM THE DARKNESS TO THE LIGHT

the ecstasy, grace and contentment
that comes from the angel of light that warms my soul?

Being away from you leaves an emptiness
in me that can only be assuaged by your presence.
Each day when I see you in my mind,
it is like I am a man with an incurable disease
who suddenly has had the holiest of women reach out,
touch me with her smile and perform a miracle cure.
I am like Lazarus rising from the dead.
You come into the dark tomb of lost hope,
tell me to "arise" and I am reborn
as I breath in the air of faith in your love for me.

Do not let discontent breed in your heart
as it sometimes appears to have been filled with doubt
and despair about that which lies ahead.
And through all this, our time together
is diminished as your weariness of heart
often precludes our conversations.
Love darling is not a primrose path
filled with scented flowers.
It is a road of curves, hills and bumps.
We are on that road now,
but I promise you at the end
of that road is a paradise of love.
I close my eyes and I see
a different place in time and space.
In my imagination I find a safe cove where
thought is unrestrained and we walk
softly on crystal clear sand
as an azure blue sea's waves gently lap at our bare feet.
We will walk the path as in a trance,
holding hands with our eyes wide open
as the cloudless skies sparkle above us.
Yes, we will walk in the paradise of our love.

LOVE: FROM THE DARKNESS TO THE LIGHT

We will feel as if we are suspended in infinity
where time is lost in a land of perfect contentment.
We will glow in the sunshine of happiness
where all our earthly cares will dissipate.
We will be beyond the hurts that we have endured
on the road to paradise.
Together we will find a sweet and perfect land
where sunbeams dance upon our heads
and where love, peace and tranquility envelope us.
From us the light of love will glow
and wonders we never dreamed possible will flow.
We will walk beyond the veil of tears
and untold joys will unfold.
Through the mists of glee we will see paradise revealed
and together we will be until
I take my last breath looking into your eyes.
Please, please, I beseech you,
take my hand darling and walk to paradise with me!

BEWTEEN MY LOVER'S LEGS
(WRITTEN IN ZESTFUL MERRIMENT
By J. Wayne Frye with Lynton Viñas)

My darling, I shall never neglect you.
You are the man who has my heart and soul.
I am yours until the end of time.
I love you with all my being so sublime.
You are the man who captured me,
And corralled my heart.
I know you feel lonely,
When we are apart.
That is because you miss me;
My twinkling eyes, my beautiful sexy body,
And my smile that destroys hearts like ancient plagues.
But who wouldn't smile
When they see what is between your legs.

LOVE: FROM THE DARKNESS TO THE LIGHT

EVEN THE HURT FEELS GOOD

I have never loved anyone like I do her.
The thought of losing her is too horrible to even consider.
I am despondent because I can't be with her.
She is on my mind day and night as I long to be with her,
to marvel at her beautiful smile,
to gaze with delight into her sparkling eyes
that twinkle like stars,
to touch her and feel the warmth
of her love, kindness and compassion,
and of course to gently kiss those succulent alluring lips
that seem to beg for attention.
I almost wish I didn't love her so much,
because it would make my life easier,
but I am so overwhelmed with love and devotion
that I ache inside for her presence.

She is so filled with kindness and love
that I ache inside when I know she is sad.
I am getting old now,
but whatever time I have left
will be devoted to her welfare,
to making her realize
that, in me, she has a champion
who will defend her honour,
and be by her side through thick and thin.
My heart beats with a rhythm of love for her
and I long to just gently stroke her soft skin
so she knows how much
I love her, desire her and pine for her.
There is an old saying: "Love hurts."
Yes, it does for both of us now,
but it is still a good feeling to know
you are loved so much,
so even the hurt feels good.

LOVE: FROM THE DARKNESS TO THE LIGHT

A VALENTINE OF LOVE FROM AFAR

There is an ocean between us.
But that cannot keep us apart.
Please know on this special day.
You have my heart.

HOW I LOVE THEE

I awake from slumber after dreaming of you.
I envision you as you travel to work.
I imagine you on a bus,
Looking out the window
At the parade of passing humanity,
Hopefully thinking of me.

I can see your brown sparkling eyes,
Your shimmering, shiny dark hair,
Your gleaming white teeth as
A gorgeous smile purses your lips,
And a flick of your head
makes your brow wrinkle.

I can sense the immense warmth
Of your deeply bronzed soft body
That bounces seductively as
The bus glides over the road.
How magnificent you look
In the glory of your womanhood.

I imagine how erotic it must feel
As you bounce up and down
Over bumps in the road
Titillating that part of your body
That is the focus of my desire
When we lie together.

LOVE: FROM THE DARKNESS TO THE LIGHT

Yet, my attraction is far
Beyond the mere sexual.
It is as if that organ is
Some mystical guide leading
To the doorway of your soul
That opens into paradise.

When I enjoy its magnificence,
I am paying homage to you.
I am trying to crawl,
Not into your body,
But into your soul,
And become one with you.

I want to melt my body,
My soul, my being
Deep with you,
So that we are one
Mentally and physically.
Oh, how I love thee.

UNTIL THE END OF TIME

I crave to take a bite of your sweetness.
I silently hunger for your love.
I crave your mouth, your voice, your hair.
Above all others you are so fair.

I hunger for your gorgeous smile.
I thirst for the nectar of your twinkling eyes.
I want to devour your soft brown skin.
I shall love you until time comes to an end.

I AM WITH YOU

There are no words I can say

LOVE: FROM THE DARKNESS TO THE LIGHT

To adequately my love convey.
How I long to touch you
And feel the warmth of your love.
You are the blood of my soul
That keeps my heart beating so bold.

Days when I cannot hear your voice,
Give me no reason to rejoice.
When I cannot see your smile,
Or the eyes that twinkle like stars
There is a deep emptiness inside
That makes me in loneliness abide.

I miss you so much I ache inside.
But within my soul you still abide.
My life is meaningless without you
To make my solemn spirits soar.
So, this special day look deep within your heart,
And know that I am with you even though we are apart

WAITING

Waiting is now a daily part of my life, because I spend hours doing just that –waiting. Let me explain. I am in love with someone in a distance land. Long distance romances are no different than romances with a person nearby. You can have arguments, although my girlfriend and I have yet to do that. You can get jealous, and we both have done that. You can laugh, share closeness of the heart, even almost reach out and touch one another through a video screen that seems to make you think you are actually physically with one another. Ah, but the waiting, that is what seems to be the bane of my existence now. When I don't get an e-mail or a Skype call from her at the usual times, I worry about her. Not calling me is like sitting at the dinner table, looking across at an empty chair and pining for the one

LOVE: FROM THE DARKNESS TO THE LIGHT

with whom you share your life. Her not being there makes my heart ache.

I have a new appreciation today for how my parents must have felt way back when they first got married, and I was gleam in my dad's eye rather than a little person sitting on my mom's lap and cooing. You see, prior to my birth, he and my mother were together for only awhile before he had to go off to war. They were apart for almost two years. How agonizing that must have been for two people in love. World War II, the Korean War, Vietnam, Afghanistan and Iraq – all the places where America, with the exception of World War II, sent its mercenaries of mayhem off to bring other nations to heel also erects a barrier between love ones who must endure separation. It is not war that separates me from my lover, but a cruel Canadian system of awarding visas only to the rich and powerful from Third World countries while allowing the "white people" from Europe and the USA in without hardly any stipulations.

I met this wonderful woman on-line and had already fallen in love after weeks of conversing with her on a daily basis. Then a few weeks ago, I flew to the Philippines to meet her. There, my love bloomed like a tulip bud opening to greet the morning sun. I like to think her love for me did the same.

I have only been apart from her a little over 4 weeks now, and all I do it seems is wait. I wait for that e-mail. I wait for that Skype call. I wait for word from my friend whom she sometimes talks with. I wait and I wait. And when that call or that e-mail doesn't come, I feel neglected. It is as if my heart has been plucked out. I feel hallow inside.

When I get that call or e-mail, it is as if a surgeon has magically transplanted a heart into the hollowness, and I

LOVE: FROM THE DARKNESS TO THE LIGHT

am once again alive. The blood is coursing through my veins and I can breathe again. I am whole.

I am like a drug addict. If I can't get my fix at the regular intervals to which I am accustomed, I feel neglected and get the shakes. I wonder why she doesn't call or e-mail. I am fragile when it comes to her love. It is as if she is my drug supplier. She is the one who feeds my habit, and each day I become more dependent on the contact I crave with her.

Love is mighty, magnificent, and too often, painful. And for me, it is also a game of waiting-waiting- waiting.

HIDDEN REQUESTS

When darkness falls and we are apart
Can love assuage a lonely heart?

I love you so intensely it hurts.
Sleep dear in peaceful repose.
With my love you are safe.
You are everything to me.
Again and again remember
I am yours forever.

Crave I your tender touch.
Your smile captivates me.
Body beautiful are you!
So remember that there is
Much of you in my heart.
I long for you day and night.

Get ready for my kisses
As an apparition of hope forms
A volcanic eruption of my love.

LOVE: FROM THE DARKNESS TO THE LIGHT

SHED NOT A TEAR

The woman I loved the most in my youth lay dying.
I thought our love could even cheat death,
but it was not to be.
By her bedside I saw my grandmother gasp for a breath
That never came, but I shed not a tear.
I was tempered by a war in a foreign land.
My 19 year old friend lay dying on wet ground.
I pleaded with him to hang on.
The end came, and I shed not a tear.
I suffered a gaping wound in my hip
From the blade of a bayonet as the foe laughed.
Blood streamed out like a raging river.
In excruciating pain, I did not shed a tear.
I have battled furiously on the hockey rink.
Tooth knocked out, jaw shattered, fingers broken,
Concussions endured for the sake of the game.
All those agonies and I shed not a tear.
I watched my dear mother battle cancer for seven years
With pain that was at times unbearable.
She finally heeded the call of eternity.
I preached her funeral, and shed not a tear.
My father lay in the hospital dying of emphysema
Almost pleading for the relief of death.
It mercifully came one dark day.
Through it all, I shed not a tear.
Today, a diminutive 5:2 woman questioned my fidelity.
I had not betrayed her, but she was unsure.
The thought of hurting her was more than I could bear.
I shed a tear! I shed a tear!

HANK WILLIAMS AND LYNTON

I used to listen to Hank Williams when I was a child, because his songs spoke of love and how it can hurt. Being

LOVE: FROM THE DARKNESS TO THE LIGHT

apart from someone you love brings loneliness and despair. I know when I long for my lover I think about how much I miss her voice, her smile, the twinkle in her eyes, her vamping, and just occasionally getting a glimpse of those gorgeous legs or getting titillated when she wears a revealing top. Being able to just gaze upon her exposed shoulders excites me. Why I asked myself are you so much in love, and the answer is always, because she is the woman for whom you have waited all your life. I am at the end of my life, but I am at the beginning of the love of my life. Upon my lover rests an awesome responsibility, because I am sailing a ship of love on the peaceful, serene waters of hope which rests in her soft hands. The below is for her.

Hank Williams Sings My Love Song

When I am without my love
The night and the day are so long
It makes me think of Hank Williams
And the world's saddest song

Did you hear that lonesome whippoorwill
He sounds too blue to fly
The midnight train is whining low
I'm so lonesome I could cry

Each word of that song
Makes me feel lonely inside
Oh, how I whine for my lover
In her arms to forever abide.

Did you ever see a night so long
When time goes crawling by
The moon just went behind the cloud
And I'm so lonesome I could cry

LOVE: FROM THE DARKNESS TO THE LIGHT

Day and night are both in darkness
Without her by my side I weep
There is an emptiness
Which I can not defeat.

Did you ever see a robin weep
When leaves begin to die
That means he's lost the will to live
And I'm so lonesome I could cry

Not hearing her sweet voice
Is a day when silence prevails
And imprisons my heart
Remembering love's little details

The silence of a falling star
Lights up a purple sky
And as I want to be where you are
I'm so lonesome I could cry

THE BODY OF MY LOVE

In the inner reaches of my mind
I see her bronze body
that glistens and glows as she
lies naked on her bed except for
a small part of the sheet that
covers her alluring breasts,
and the wrinkled lower sheet that
hides that heavenly delight that lies
between those gorgeous silky thighs.

She has her hands clasped
behind her curly hair
exposing the soft hair of her underarms
that is dark with sensual delight,

LOVE: FROM THE DARKNESS TO THE LIGHT

and seems to longingly plead for
the gentle blowing of my breath.
Her body appears to long for
my loving benevolent embrace.
She is soft like Belgium lace.

When eve-tide falls
I dream of her soft skin and am
forged like a weapon of love.
I am an arrow of affection that
wants to pierce her soul.
I long to sip from the goblet
of delight between her soft thighs,
because it is the nectar of my life.
It sooths all my strife.

It is the body of the woman I love.
She quenches my thirst.
She feeds my hunger.
She satisfies my boundless desire.
Yet, in all her sensuous delight
I am appeased more by that
which is simple upon my eyes.
That gorgeous smile that glows
with love for me that so gently flows.

As mentioned previously, with Lynton you get a package deal, as her wonderful friends Ingrid and Channa are an important part of her life; and therefore; also become a part of the life of anyone lucky enough to share Lynton's love. So, the following poem was written in praise of two women who shared a fun day shopping for a present I bought for Lynton. In fact, it eventually led to the second book in my Lynton series about a sinister element that invades the girl's lives and leads to them tackling demons in an old haunted house.

LOVE: FROM THE DARKNESS TO THE LIGHT

LYNTON AND CHANNA GO SHOPPING

One Saturday in the land of heat,
Two girls to Manila town did go.
One was beautiful, prim and proper.
The other short, beautiful, and darkly scintillating.
The mall was their destination,
Where like two bees they hummed.
Watch out men, you might get stung.

They both had a gorgeous smile.
Channa bought clothes for style.
Lynton, though, wanted a cell phone.
Quick, she thought, I have to
Buy it before my money is gone.
But Channa grabbed her by the hand
And said, spend Wayne's money in happy land.

Shop, shop, shop, shop.
They shopped till they dropped
Shop, shop, shop, shop.
They just could not seem to stop.
Channa moved about with glee,
Gyrating with precision in the mall,
Her shapely form for all to see.

Her credit was at the top
Her spending going up, up.
She paid with cash or credit card,
And begged Lynton for Wayne's money
To spend, because for her the
Wild spending knew no end.
Over the edge did she descend.

Shop, shop, shop, shop.
Lynton shouts you have to stop.

LOVE: FROM THE DARKNESS TO THE LIGHT

Wayne will get so mad.
You and I will wind up sad.
Shamed by her spending,
Channa bows to sanity now.
She makes a courtly vow.

Shop, shop, shop, shop
These girls realize Wayne may call a cop.
Shop, shop, shop, shop.
Their spending makes a big drop!
The phone is purchased and a call is made.
"Hey, Wayne guess what?
We spent all you got."
Give us some more and
We will buy a yacht.

No relationship is entirely smooth, and despair can briefly rear its ugly head as doubt prevails. Still, the trials and tribulations can serve as a solidifying catalyst to strengthen a relationship rather than destroy it.

THE FAITHFUL HEART IN THE ZIGZAG OF TIME

Wayne stood on the burning deck of despair.
Whence it appeared his lover had fled;
The flame that lit his heart was a flickering wreck,
Floating like a vapour all about his head.
Yet bold and bright he stood,
As born to rule the love storm;
True love coursing through his blood,
He sought Lynton in magnificent form.
The flames rolled on, but he would not go
Without Lynton's soft word;
He could sense death below,
Her voice no longer heard.
With hope, faith and affection fair,

LOVE: FROM THE DARKNESS TO THE LIGHT

That well had borne their part
                The noblest thing which perished there
Was that dependent faithful heart.

Sex is a part of any loving romantic relationship, and although it is certainly an important part of love, if it is all there is, love is simply misplaced desire and lust. However, I like to have fun by using sex as an innuendo of mirth.

HER LOVE SETS ME FREE

She is like the raging fires of Taal.
A volcano that represents my desire.
She shakes my body
with quakes of delight.
I sit and wait for her,
because she is my light.

The fires inside me rage all about.
Like Taal I burn with desire for her.
She is my heaven on earth.
I quiver each time I see her smile.
My heart is on alert.

I can feel an explosion of love.
She envelopes me in hot fire.
I burn with great glee.
I shiver and shake because
her love sets me free.

LEGS OF DESIRE

Her brown skin sends ripples of desire
Through my mind that longs for her.
Sparkling brown eyes twinkle with delight
In the picture she gave me.

LOVE: FROM THE DARKNESS TO THE LIGHT

Between my legs I feel a tingle in the night.

I gaze ever downward at her legs
That seem to glisten with sensuality.
In my furtive mind they are dancing
A steady rhythm that gets my libido
Erect and prancing, prancing, prancing.

Oh, those firm fitting shorts
That hug her body so tight
Make me feel a raging fire
That consumes me up and down
As I am filled with burning desire.

The watch on her wrist is envied by me,
Because it can feel her pulse.
How I long to touch those gorgeous legs
And linger in such delight.
My desire for her pulsates and begs.

Those legs, those silky smooth legs
Are the limbs of a mighty tree
That stands tall in my mind.
Oh desire be stilled
To my heart be kind.

My gaze always is on her legs.
One touch, one smooth stroke
Of that delicate soft skin
Would make me beg to
Commit a physical sin.

A tender kiss I would give.
A kiss delicate with love.
That would linger there
Upon that which I desire,

LOVE: FROM THE DARKNESS TO THE LIGHT

On her legs so fair.

I CLOSED THE DOOR

I waited on her kiss,
I waited for her embrace;
I waited on her lips,
I waited on her excuse,
I waited on her apology,
But I am not waiting anymore.

I'm not waiting on her kiss,
I'm not waiting on her embrace,
I'm not waiting on her lips,
I'm not waiting on her excuse.
I'm not waiting on her apology.
I'm simply disinterested now.

I have found a woman who
Stirs my wondering soul.
I wait for her kiss.
I wait for her embrace.
I wait for her soft lips.
I wait for her to put
Her jealousy aside,

Her love is genuine.
Ah, I want her to know
Now I have found
That which has eluded me
In a life of searching.

The door to the old love closed
Like a steel trap in a dungeon.
For, I have found respite
In the arms of she

LOVE: FROM THE DARKNESS TO THE LIGHT

Who lifts my spirit
And makes me whole.
I long for her.
I pine for her.
I want her to know
That she who once had me
Will never have me anymore,
Because I have closed that door.

IT IS LYNTON I LOVE

How do you know when
You are truly in love?
Well, when push comes to shove
Your libido can be the judge.
It is a barometer of your feelings.
It has an answer for any misgivings.

In the near and distant past,
Even though I loved my wife,
A roving eye could often cause strife.
My fidelity was never in question,
But how I used to get a tingle,
When with attractive women I would mingle.

Today I was strolling on the promenade
That winds through the downtown,
And there was something interesting I found.
When a woman flirted with me,
I did not get that old familiar tingle.
I had no earthly urge to mingle.

Gone are the days when I look
At women with apparent lust,
For now a mighty surge does not gust.
What once aroused and titillated

LOVE: FROM THE DARKNESS TO THE LIGHT

Is now stayed from above,
Because it is Lynton I love.

SONG OF LOVE

I am sorry you cry like you do.
I never want to hurt you.
Know strife will never last.
Together our lot is cast.

I ache inside and I am scared too.
I never want to see you blue.
But there is one thing that is forever true.
Eventually, forever I will be with you.

COME TO PARADISE WITH ME

Your femininity overwhelms me
Your steady strength supports me
Your tenderness sustains me,
Your perfect love comforts me.
Come my love to paradise with me.

HEAVEN'S DELIGHT

I can't tell you how sorry I am
To have questioned the love I have found.
My heart is aching with remorse.
I wish I could take it back
What I said of course.

You know that I am extremely sorry though,
And I will work hard to defeat the jealousy foe.
I will be forever very contrite,
Because in you I have found
The glory and hope of heaven's delight.

LOVE: FROM THE DARKNESS TO THE LIGHT

DEPTH OF LOVE

I love you more than you
could ever comprehend
I love you so much that
I no longer know where you end and I begin,
because I feel like I never lived
before I had you.
I was only existing.
The hours I spend with you
I look upon as sort of a perfumed garden,
a dim twilight in the garden of good
where a fountain of love pours out of me.
You and you alone make me feel that I am alive.
I need not ever go to heaven,
because in your arms, I am already there!

PLEASE DON'T MAKE ME A POOR MAN

Only you turning your back on me,
giving up on our relationship can destroy my love for you,
and even then I would continue loving you,
because you are the last love of my live,
and I want to take my last breath in your arms,
knowing that my life with you was heaven,
because when I am in your arms,
when I look into your eyes,
when I feel your soft flesh,
when I hear your melodic voice,
when I see that captivating smile
I believe in God, because to me you are God!
Please be with me and let me pray to you,
pray for your love,
because it is the only thing of value in my life.
Without that I am spiritually broke.
Please don't make me a poor man!

LOVE: FROM THE DARKNESS TO THE LIGHT

THE FIRES OF LOVE

When at first sight I fell into your lair,
My heart was filled with a raging fire.
If she loves me I said, that is all I need.
I will have a lifetime of promises and dreams,
For my heart now knows what love means.

THE LOVE IN YOUR HEART

As you sleep peacefully, I sit here and long for you.
That is my destiny - to long for you the rest of my life,
to long for your warmth and for your love,
because it is what sustains me.
Whenever I want to feel lifted in spirit,
Whenever I want to sense the majesty of hope,
for a better and glorious tomorrow,
I reflect on music that reaches
the heart and makes you realize
that there is goodness within you
that will rise to the surface
and break through despair.
. I have found myself because of the love
of a woman filled with love, kindness and generosity.
I now here the symphony of life.
. It is the music of my life.
It is music of the heart and soul
that makes me long for
your caresses, your kisses, for the softness of your body,
and above all, for the love in your heart.

FRIEND AND LOVER

How wonderful to be accepted as a friend
by your glorious lover.
What greater honour to be friend and lover.

LOVE: FROM THE DARKNESS TO THE LIGHT

If I could reach up and hold a star
for every time you have made me smile,
the entire sky would be in the palm of my hand.
A part of you has grown in me.
It is you and I now rather than "me,"
and though an ocean may be between us,
there is no distance in my heart.
I can sense your beauty.
I can imagine your kindness.
I can see that captivating smile
that lights up the darkness in
the furtive recesses of my mind.
I can feel your warmth and grace
as if you were by my side.
You are the bright beacon of hope
that shines brightly to guide me
to paradise in your arms.

FOREVER

I had been lost in a tyranny of despair.
I knew no laughter, my happiness gone.
Lowering my head, I looked at a blank wall.
Meeting you, I stopped looking back.
I ceased scowling at my fate.
Now, I desire my dust to be mingled with yours
Forever and forever and forever.

THE INTERLUDE

Be still my pounding heart.
Though we are still far apart,
My lover called me on skype.
My loneliness to boldly fight.
Looking upon her for a short time,
Brought back memories so sublime

LOVE: FROM THE DARKNESS TO THE LIGHT

Of when we talked hours during the day
As we had so much to say.
I gazed upon her beautiful face,
My heart strings feeling like fine lace.
My billowed soul with love soared.
A mighty river of affection was forged.
Her soft moist lips tantalized me,
Making me tingle where eyes cannot see.
Warm and sincere, I felt her love within,
Knowing between us nothing can be a sin.
The connection broke and she is gone,
But the love she showed never leaves me alone.
One act of kindness she earnestly pursued.
Ah, what a fantastic romantic interlude.

MY ANGEL LEFT HER WINGS IN MY HEART

I have this angel who in my heart left her wings.
She has no idea how much happiness she truly brings.
Within me is a light for her which shines so bright.
My pride in her gives me such great delight.

Her demeanour is sweet, soft and pure.
Sometimes she can be wilful and sometimes she is demure.
She tries her very hardest to please and do what's right.
She sorrows for those who hunger at night.

Everyone sees this light within her soul.
In this world, she plays her unheralded role.
She is considerate to everyone she knows.
The light within shines brighter as my angel grows.

When she sees someone suffer, it opens up her heart.
She wants to do all that she can; she wants to do her part.
She'll squeeze my sorrow and make me forget the pain.
She shows me where the sun is when I suffer the rain.

LOVE: FROM THE DARKNESS TO THE LIGHT

I know no God, but I can sense her special grace.
I bow before my own providence seeing my angel's face.
And in that very moment when she came into my world
I knew that she was so much more than just my loving girl.

She is my sunshine, with a sweetness that will not end.
Her righteousness I will boldly defend.
She is the reason I always try my best.
Oh, my love for her passes the test.

As I face my mortality each and every day,
And in my grave I shall eventually lay,
I treasure her like gold piled in a cart.
Yes, my angel left her wings in my heart.

A VOLCANO OF LOVE

With a seething cauldron more furious
than when the mighty Taal is a raging inferno,
a mountain of love burns deep within me.
My affection for her clear for all to see.
Rising vapours of affection pour from my soul,
spewing red hot molten lava filled with passion,
spilling down a mountainside of adoration.

Motivated by three extraordinary women called Lynton, Ingrid and Channa, I wrote a book series featuring them as brave heroines in the fight for justice. In LYNTON BUYS A NEW CELL PHONE AND HEARS THE VOICE OF DOOM, these three girls go up against cruel demons in a haunted house where evil has taken up residence. The battle is an allegory for all the ills of a society based on greed and how a few good people can stand against the tyranny that relegates the many in servitude the few who have lives of grandiose splendour built on the backs of the poor. What follows are poems and an short excerpt that are

LOVE: FROM THE DARKNESS TO THE LIGHT

indicative how the power of love can overcome adversity in a world where compassion is in short supply.

COWER DEMONS BEFORE THE RIGHTEOUS

The daughters of hope
Cannot be consumed by flames.
They march against demons.
Purity pumps from their hearts
In veins of molten rock
To tear demons apart.
Storms of their purity prevail.
These girls vow not to fail.
Be careful their ire not to rile.
Lava pours like the falling rains,
Quakes of determination spew forth,
Shaking them free of demon chains.

They ride forth on horses of hope,
Steeds born of angelic untaintedness.
They await the call to gather arms
For war that tethers against fate.
Swords held high with righteous fury
These women fight for love's sake.
The darkness of hell blights
out the brightness of day,
With evil gloomy shadows spreading
From demons seeking souls.
These princesses of light
Are bold and ready to fight.
Do not mistake their womanliness
With a lack of verve and determinedness.
They fear no demons of the night,
For they carry the righteous light.
So cower you demons of the dark.
These three can destroy you with one spark.

LOVE: FROM THE DARKNESS TO THE LIGHT

Continuing in this vain, I offer the below two ditties as a tribute to these three extraordinary women who came into my life and, as friends to my dear Lynton, embraced me and made me feel loved at a time when I was floundering in a sea of misery swirling about in a tempestuous storm of discontent. What an incredibly lucky man I was to find one woman who showered me with love, and along with her, two others who reached out to me in harmonious friendship.

IN THE GARDEN OF THREE GODDESSES

The blazing eye of dawn lights the day
as joy before mortals lay.
These three shine heaven's light
as their beauty takes flight.

Their veils parted, the earth bows
giving way to shades of blue and gold.
These three shine like polished steel
in the noonday sun brazen and bold.

Planted in their garden are great delights.
The leafs of trees rustle lightly in the breeze,
whispering their praises in harmonious flights,
before the sunlight serenely flees.

Their realm is eternal and flawless
as clay and earth and blade of grass
stretch forth to feel the loving light
that glistens like sparking brass.

Untainted, pure of heart, with spirits of hope,
three Goddesses dance in the Sunday sun
dangling passions beauteous alluring rope
and before all the world their seductive web is spun.

LOVE: FROM THE DARKNESS TO THE LIGHT

POETRY IN MOTION

There are three friends that came into my life,
They stayed the blindness of dust in my eye,
They all went south and east and north.
But with one of them I shall stay until I die.

These three friends that spoke of the dead.
They said the strong man fights but the sick man dies.
"And you who embraced us three," they said,
"Put the sun in our face and happiness in our eyes."

Oh, can anyone be as lucky as I?
Who is loved by one of the three,
But now revered by each one
The whole world joyously can see.

I revel in joy that they have each other.
I bow before their strong devotion,
And realize that their friendship
Is poetry in motion.

ADORATION

The meaning of being special,
is found in a person like you.
A woman who seeks love,
in everything you say and do.

A person who betters my life,
by being a part of it each day.
Someone who touches my heart,
in a special and unique way.
A person who is always giving,
and who helps others all the time.
Who truly gives from the heart,

LOVE: FROM THE DARKNESS TO THE LIGHT

showing they care so sublime.

Happiness I have found in you.
A woman who is all she could be.
I am so blessed to have you in my life
I adore you it is so easy to see.

LITTLE ACTS

Don't leave the world you desire high and dry.
Believe that you can be the person you want to be.
Believe in the kindness of strangers.
You have not lived a perfect day,
Unless you help someone
Who will never be able to repay.
The best portions of a good person's life
Are the little nameless acts of kindness and love.

EXCERPT FROM
LYNON BUYS A NEW CELL PHONE
AND HEARS THE VOICE OF DOOM

Lynton gripped the cell-phone. No, she caressed it as if it was her life-link to Wayne. She was thinking how much her love for Wayne had grown since its purchase. She and Wayne had learned much about each other since the cell-phone purchase only a few days ago. It had led to consternation because of neglect, suspicions and uncertainty. Yet their relationship was stronger now. Their troubles had started over Wayne's insecurities and lack of trust. He accused Lynton of deception, but any deception from her was not about a lack of love. It was about her need to deal with her own suspicions about Wayne. She had endured pain without telling him, because she wanted to be magnanimous and understanding, but how could anyone understand about Wayne spending a week with his ex-wife under the same roof. Then going to a hotel where they had rooms across the hall from one another. And she had even seen her come into Wayne's room as if she belonged there. The whole time Lynton was in pain, suffering with anxiety and fears that he might once again return to the familiar and discard the new. Her lack of communication with Wayne had made him agonize over what he might have done without realizing that his insensitivity was a major factor. She had never been unresponsive before. So, he, for the first time, found reasons to doubt her over the appearing and disappearing contact telephone numbers which obviously meant she was talking to other men. Why shouldn't she? Wayne had spent a week and a half with his ex-wife. Yet, they had talked their way through it, and Wayne had simply decided that there was absolutely no reason to continue to beat a dead horse. What had been done had been done. He told Lynton that it no longer mattered, because their love had pulled them through trying times.

Like the wind whistling incessantly through the dark nights of loneliness, time carries away the deeds of uncertainty and with those who love deeply, the uncertainty fades into a soft stream that meanders through valleys, hills and plains to flow into a lake of harmoniousness. The pain Wayne felt with jealous uncertainty had been assuaged, not by any admission from Lynton, but by her pleading that she was a good girl who had done nothing wrong despite appearances. She was so kind, so gentle, so caring, so sincere that Wayne's heart melted with empathy for a woman who had endured poverty, pain and misery in her life, but only desired to find the right man to make her feel loved and wanted in a world which was often hostile to her. She had found that in Wayne. And in her, Wayne had found the woman who would lift him from despair and guide him into the paradise of her arms.

LOVE: FROM THE DARKNESS TO THE LIGHT

GLORIFIED WOMAN

For me there lies within the lights
and shadows of your eyes,
the beauty of your soul.
I see not the exterior
But the interior that glistens
with abiding goodness.
That is the woman I love.
This is the woman I glorify
in the far reaches of my mind.

As a writer, I recall experiences to catalogue that which may make for good prose. Seeing the evil that lurks about every day in a world where only the few seem to get the good things in life, I agonize for economic and social justice. With that in mind, when I wrote the story about three women battling demons, it seemed an allegorical statement that used the demons as metaphors for the capitalistic system where there can only be glorified winners at the top if there are those who are permanently relegated to the bottom. The evil house mentioned below is a metaphor for capitalism.

THE EVIL HOUSE ACROSS THE WAY

Across the street is a lonely house I know
That became evil many a summer ago,
And left no trace of love within its walls,
And there no daylight falls.
It is where evil incubates and grows.

Its shrubs from prying eyes are a shield.
Are there ghosts there afield;
The old man living there looks like a corpse,
And eerie sounds within abound.

LOVE: FROM THE DARKNESS TO THE LIGHT

There is an abiding evil to the sound.

I look at it with an aching heart.
I cannot from it feel far apart.
On that disused and forgotten path
There seems a beckoning call
That will make evil night fall.
The ravens flitter overhead and shout,
And a hush of death is all about.
I hear the devil from across the way
To have his evil say,
And take souls for pay.
It is under the small, dim star.
I know not what evils there are
Who share the unlit place within me,
Like stones under the low-limbed tree.
Oh, my soul, the evil there it does see.

That house is whining and sad.
It knows no modern fad.
From there no one ever sings
In the view of so many things.
It is as if the house had fangs.

THE SIMPLE GIRL

She calls herself a simple girl.
She does not ask for much from life.
Just to love and be loved.
She works hard and strives
For perfection of the soul.
Her hair is radiant and black.
She never keeps it in place,
Flipping it around like soft lace.

Her mood is always gregariously fine.

LOVE: FROM THE DARKNESS TO THE LIGHT

This girl makes me walk the line.
Feeling her love fills me with glee.
She strives her love for me to see.
Each day I awaken to her call,
As without it my spirits will fall.
Oh my, I burn with raging desire,
Because she sits my heart on fire.

LOVE ACROSS SPACE AND TIME

Tonight I made love with an angel lost in time.
Ah, how she coaxed me with her wiles so fine.
Though distance precluded a real touch,
the Internet made it possible her heart to clutch.
Kindred love reached beyond space and time,
as we explored a distance induced caress,
searching for the soul's most tender place.
Her words smouldered like embers in coal.
Oh, she set my love-worn heart ablaze.
Her sultry words enflamed fantasies craze.

So eloquent was she that when I closed my eyes
I could feel deep within her seductive touch.
I could even inhale the scent of her ethereal rush.
The things she said made my passion rise.
Between us please let there never be lies.
Could she hear my soft whispers and gentle moans?
Oh, she was an ocean away in a distant land,
but everything seemed so absolute and real.
She made love to me every way a heart desires,
looking at her kindled within me raging fires.
Yes, I made love to an angel so fine.
Please let her truly be mine.

Now, those bastions of probity who like to discount sex as a glorious part of love live in a world where the anatomy of

LOVE: FROM THE DARKNESS TO THE LIGHT

the make and female is abhorred and looked upon as evil manifestations of human's lustful nature. What is wrong with lusting after he or she whom you love? It is as natural as breathing air or drinking water. So, what follows is a natural reaction to love.

THE ARDOUR BETWEEN MY LEGS

I adore her pallor and her dress.
Above all I adore her beautiful new tress
That sparkles and dances in the light.
As down below begins a rise I cannot fight.

It is as dark as coal her hair
Not tarnished or filled with nature's rust.
She is young and ever so fair.
Below it rises like a spectre from dust.

Oh noble woman so dark and true,
I adore the new sheen to your hair,
That flutters about like morning dew,
My, the methodical rise hastens there.

You hair floats about like autumn leaves,
And I long to touch it so fair.
It is the tangled dew falling on golden sheaves.
Now, there is a real tingle down there.

Silken threads of charcoal black
My ardour moves up and up,
As I think of that beautiful crack.
Down below the passion will fill a cup.

Tresses float down to her small bosom there,
And I long to suckle like a newborn so fair.
Oh, I beg to take her to our rented lair,

LOVE: FROM THE DARKNESS TO THE LIGHT

And watch what's between my legs rise into the air.

Her locks as dark as the raven's wing,
Make me want to chant and sing.
The passion is like a religious belief.
Oh my, down below comes sweet relief.
Her hair is used to entice and vamp.
I am proud I rose up like a champ,
But now what her ardour has built
Between my legs begins to wilt.

SHE SHINES LIKE A LIGHT ABOVE

Shakespeare was a man of great words,
that were masked in allegorical whimsy.
I know not his verve and depth,
and I use flowing phrases but am clumsy.

I look upon your face,
and think the moon in it shines
as against a crimson night
my heart fills with love's lines.

When the wind gently kisses the trees,
as they make no noise on such a night,
I think of the walls I must climb
just to see your radiant light.

On many a lonely night nigh of you
I weep waiting for your lover's dew.
Like a lion's roar with such incredible might,
you come into view and renew my sight.

On such a night as this, I long
for your warm, kind, loving embrace.
Ah, how my heart sings a lover's song,

LOVE: FROM THE DARKNESS TO THE LIGHT

as I envision your soft, lovely face.

Clouds cover the stars of night,
and I steal alone in search of you.
Loneliness I must desperately fight,
so desperation does not spew.
On such a night your glow is felt,
as inside my heart does melt
to never slander that which I love
that shines like a light above.

ETERNITY'S KISS

I want to hold you in the kitchen
I want to fondle you in the living room.
I want to grope in the bedroom.
I want to swivel you so profound,
So I can turn you around,
And whisper loves sound.

In my arms there is now wrong,
As I lace fingers through your hair.
I will hold you tight as I kiss your cheek.
I want you to look into my eyes
So my love you can inhale,
While I light passions trail.

I long to savour that which I adore.
My ardour for you will longingly soar.
My lips will nary a crevice miss.
Vibrations of my desire
Will slowly climb upwards
As I am consumed with fire.

I want to hear your moaning and sighs
As your loveliness below me lies.

LOVE: FROM THE DARKNESS TO THE LIGHT

The melding of two lives we will assert.
Ah, you will make me stand alert.
I will devour you like a four course meal,
Chewing, kissing, licking where you appeal.
Your smell is like frankincense and myrrh.
You warm me like a fox's fur.
You let me touch where others don't dare.
Oh, that one spot I adore is so fair.
Living for you is my life's fondest reason,
Because you have released me from prison.
I want to lie by your side as if to pray
My hands under your knees as I lay.
Lifting them atop my shoulders
As I go lower and lower.
Let my tongue write a message with each brush,
Slowly because worshipping you is such a rush.

Kissing from your belly to your head,
I feel your indomitable pleasure spread.
I am only safe in your grasp.
Our love will forever last.
I rise from oblivion for your caress.
Loving you is my life I confess.

We are a somersault of love within
Between us there is no sin.
Where does all this love end?
Each day is as it was when we began.
Forever in ethereal, starry bliss
Together we shall sweet eternity kiss.

THE RHYTHM OF LOVE

I open the door to the salon.
I look toward the back where she sits.
She rises gracefully like the morning sun.

LOVE: FROM THE DARKNESS TO THE LIGHT

She shines radiantly as she glides toward me
Like a gazelle on the plains of Africa.
Each stride is a motion of poetry.
The sway of the hips is enticing.
The motion of her shoulders reared back in confidence
As she moves toward me belying a woman of pride.
Ah, and between my legs is that tingle that only she
Can bring to a man who is smitten and devoured by
Her glorious beauty that titillates and arouses.
My pounding heart cannot be staid by
The rhythm of love that overwhelms me.

SHE MAKES ME TINGLE

I walk into your place of work.
I see your enticing feet in high heels.
You glide like a gazelle toward me.
I quiver between my legs at your sight.
I am too old for this I tell myself,
But the tingle won't go away.
Oh, how I want to strip you bare
And take you to our lover's lair.
Ah, you take my breath away.
What else can I possibly say.

SWEET NECTAR OF THE WOMAN I LOVE

Last night passed in your usual delight.
You let me savour your nectar without protest.
Swallowing your essence filled me with joy.
Oh its sweet smell. Its sweet taste.
Having sucked deep in a peonies' delight
Your sweet honey seeped out of its hairy recesses
And filled me with hope that I may always
Worship your womanliness that stands in grandeur
Before the altar of the Gods.

LOVE: FROM THE DARKNESS TO THE LIGHT

THE WINGS OF AN ANGEL IN HUMAN FORM

Each morning I awake with an angel by my side.
Her bounty is as boundless as the endless sea.
Her love is the smoke raised from burning embers
That sparkle and crackle with tranquil hope.
Things base and vile have no place in her world,
As she shines and glows with the light of promise.
When love speaks from her succulent, moist lips
It is the voice of a Goddess that makes
Heaven drowsy with harmonious envy
That one of its angels descended from on high
And became a human to lie by my side.

WELCOME MY LOVE AND FAREWELL MY LOVE

My heart was beating, swiftly like a tired horse,
As across a crowded room I spotted you and was done.
Already evening cradled earth's course,
Night came as the light disappeared with the sun.
Like a strong oak I stood, yes I stood,
A vast giant, towering upwards there,
Where from out the shadowy wood
A hundred dark eyes seemed to stare.

From a bank of cloud the moon gazed,
Sadly out of the mist about her,
The winds beat soft wings, and strayed
Around a melody in my ears:
The night begot a thousand monsters,
But my spirit was joyful, lively:
Deep inside my veins what fire!
Deep inside my heart what heat!

I saw you, and full measure of bliss
Flowed to me from your sweet eyes:

LOVE: FROM THE DARKNESS TO THE LIGHT

I drew for you my every breath,
My heart was wholly on your side.
You filled my life with a glow, it shone
All about your lovely face, lit
Tenderly for me – dear woman!
I had your love, but not deserved.

But ah, finally at one morning's light
My heart was crushed in bitter parting:
In your kisses I would no longer delight!
In your eyes I saw I caused suffering!
I cried, you stood, looked from above,
And saw me go from your gaze:
And yet what joy it was to be loved!
To be loved by you - what happiness!

Thus we have had to dwell apart
In lands so different and far away,
Making our love sometimes smart.
Still, to be loved by you is a gift
And deep within my sorrow
Does your abiding love vigorously lift,
For I know I shall have you tomorrow.

THE SPARK WITHIN

At times the light of hope is extinguished,
but it is often rekindled from a spark
that comes along at the most unexpected time.
Be forever grateful to those who rekindle
that flame you thought was lost deep within.

SONG OF LYNTON

If have gone across the ocean to the Philippines
Where I sit and watch the closing of each day,

LOVE: FROM THE DARKNESS TO THE LIGHT

Looking out on humid, steamy Manila Bay.
Just to hear the rumble of a Jeepney,
Makes me feel like I am resting on hay.
I pass the time of the day,
Waiting for she who has captured my heart.

The breeze blows gently through the air,
As I wait the arrival of she who is so fair.
She is like a candle glowing in the dark,
And within my heart she leaves her mark.
I do not worry about a life hereafter
For now I have made my heaven on earth
In the warm arms of she who gave me rebirth.

DISTANT DRUMS OF LOVE

In the words of that old Jim Reeves song,
I hear, yes I hear the sound of distant drums.
They are calling me to you
To share all the time we can before my end.

Love me now my love,
For we know not how long we have.
Please take my hand and join me,
Join me in the calm of a silken sea.

I hear the sound of Gabriel's trumpet blow.
Can it be far away, far away?
If he calls, I will not go.
For in your arms I long to stay.

Savour each minute, do not wait,
For distant drums may change our fate.
Love me now, for time is ticking,
And it may be all we have.

LOVE: FROM THE DARKNESS TO THE LIGHT

The hands on a clock click, click, click.
And it sounds like distant drums, distant drums.
Rest in my arms and feel my love
As we hear the sound of distant drums, distant drums.

DOING LAUNDRY AS AN ACT OF LOVE

One thing you learn in the Philippine Islands
Is that things are done incredibly different here.
Antiquated methods make washing clothes no easy task,
And my dear lover shakes her head and says
"Don't do it baby, you'll throw your back out I fear."

I learned long ago that little things are what show love.
Today, I threw caution to the wind and defied her.
I swirled the blue detergent in the cap of the bottle
And poured it in the washer with great care,
Then stood and listened to the washing machine purr.

As I sat the timer, the soap reminded me of sand,
Small grains picked up on a beach flowing through a hand.
Falling to the ground, the ocean sweeps them away.
Life is like that, fleeting, as it is, makes you realize
We must all make the most of each and every day.

I look down at the tiles on the floor thinking of love.
It is the little things that matter when push comes to shove.
Now I am so frightened, because I defied the little dynamo.
Will she say "thank you" or deliver a crushing right hand,
And send his poor Canadian boy to the Promised Land?

SEX AND LOVE

Sex with you is a celebration of my love.
I take great pleasure in giving you pleasure.

LOVE: FROM THE DARKNESS TO THE LIGHT

Feeling your pulsating orgasm each morning
Fills me with more than your orgasmic delight
It fills me with you, and when I hear you sigh with pleasure
I feel all warm inside and euphoric.
It spreads harmonious waves through my body,
not because of my orgasm, but because of yours.
Every caress, every touch, ever glance, every soft whisper
is my way of letting you know how much you mean to me.
Sex with you is not a mechanical act,
it is a performance of love,
and a continuum of the attraction you have for me.
I hope one day you will understand that
my physical attraction to you is not about sex.
It is about how much I want every part of you to be mine,
and how bringing you pleasure, bringing you happiness
affords me the greatest joy imaginable.

NEW LOVE, NEW LIFE

Heart, my heart, what can it mean?
What could make you beat just so?
What a strange new life, it seems!
Gone is that I used to know.
The sad past is over and done,
Everything that grieved me,
All the heartache is now gone –
My happiness abounds for all to see!

I am trapped by her lovely youth
By that beloved form,
By those eyes so good and true,
By that all-powerful force?
I could never run away,
Collect myself and flee,
My path never varies or strays
It is love of her you see.

LOVE: FROM THE DARKNESS TO THE LIGHT

She has bound me with magic thread, so
Even with distance it cannot be untied,
The dear girl with an infectious smile, oh
She holds me fast: and I
Must lie within her magic spell
And live where she may go.
How great the change, I tell!
Love! Love! Never let me go!

THE GODDESS OF LIGHT IN MY LIFE

As time goes on,
we men often realize
that the special woman in our life
is a Goddess of hope in a sea of turmoil.
We are lucky to be greeted every day
at the door with
a mischievous, slow smile that
gradually spreads across thick,
succulent, ruby red lips
from a woman who shines
as if the light around her
is ghost-like, condensed
as if she were a lithe gazelle
slanting with precision
ready to leap across the plain.
She is a sleek racing yacht,
sailing upon the deep blue waters of lust,
and she exudes peace and serenity
that soothes us in the warmth of her arms.
She is the bright North Star
that is the beacon of navigation
leading to sanguine peacefulness.
She is the sunlight that comes up
on the morning horizon,
the soft cool breeze that

LOVE: FROM THE DARKNESS TO THE LIGHT

floats gently across the undulating waves
and makes them ripple with
anticipatory delight at her carnal collaborations.
The foam of her sweet, soft voice
flies like flaky snow before
the wintry tempest of temptation.
The brightness of her sparkling eyes
sets a course towards tranquility
in a calm sea that radiates
with her golden haze
that glistens and glows.
Thus is the Goddess of light in our lives.

GOODBYE FOR AWHILE

There is something inside me
I cannot deny.
It will hurt me deeply
to tell you good-bye.

I know I'll only be gone a month.
Why do I feel so sad?
Why does the thought of leaving
make me feel so bad?

I will miss your arms
that hold me so tight.
I will miss your kisses,
miss holding you at night.

I will miss your laugh
and that gorgeous smile,
Even though I am leaving
for only a short while.

You've become my light in darkness,

LOVE: FROM THE DARKNESS TO THE LIGHT

casting your glow like the moon.
I depend on your love,
So I will be back soon!
I am leaving behind my heart,
And our growing memories too
of the times that we've shared
and please know I love you.

SHE BRINGS COMFORT

She is sitting here with me now.
Although sometimes we might go 15 minutes
without a word spoken, just feeling
her presence brings comfort to me.

How does one describe perfection?
Is it in a the smile she flashes
when she walks in from work?
Is it the gleam in her eyes
when she looks at me?
Is it the way she snuggles up
to me at night when we lie down?
Is it the mischievous giggle that bounces about?

She is what makes my sun shine.
She is the sparkle in my diamond.
She is the beacon of hope
when I am in despair.
She is the flickering candle
that brightens the darkness.
She is the signpost of joy
on the road to blissfulness.

She is sitting here with me now.
Although sometimes we might go 15 minutes
without a word spoken, just feeling

LOVE: FROM THE DARKNESS TO THE LIGHT

her presence brings comfort to me.

> Love is the main course. Sex is the dessert.

I CANNOT COMPREHEND WHY SHE LOVES ME

Are you sure you want me?
Hurry now, I'll only count to three.
Then, you'll be stuck forever with me.
I want you to be my Mrs.
And I will shower you with kisses.

I looked in the mirror today
And there is something I have to say.
Why would a beautiful woman like you
Want an old man as withered as the dew?
Surely you can do better than me.

My breasts are bigger than Dolly Parton's.
My belly could fill up a thousand cartons.
Sex with me is less than appealing.
If you find it, you know what you are feeling?
Consider the hand I am dealing.

I understand how I am not alluring in the night?
Why even in the daytime I am a dreadful sight.
Penetrating you would be a delight,
But thinking of that horrible sight.
Makes want to turn off the light.

I am a realist, who does not want a broken heart,
So, please do not eventually pierce it with a dart,
And my intrepid soul deeply sear.
Just let me know now if I displease you my dear.
I will bow my head and calmly disappear.

LOVE: FROM THE DARKNESS TO THE LIGHT

SMILE LITTLE GIRL

Smile my little girl,
As in me you awaken
The most glorious world,
If I'm not mistaken.
Kiss your adoring lover,
Dance a sweet measure,
Find your name in my heart,
With all its buried treasure
Face your life knowing love
Its pain, its pleasure,
For the depth of my love
Is impossible to measure.

SHINE IN MY HEART

She is calm and sweet.
She sings like a nightingale
For hundreds who intently listen.
But for me, she sings a tune
Full of liquid moonlight
And uses the twinkling stars
To shine into my heart.

THE BREEZE OF LOVE

She sleeps now in sweet repose.
I am still basking in the after-glow
From our conversation an hour ago,
When her sweet voice and image
Lifted my spirits that were low.

How does one properly say
Thanks to an angel who shines a light
That fills your heart with celestial delight.

LOVE: FROM THE DARKNESS TO THE LIGHT

She is the star in the heavens above
That makes my life so right.

So sleep softly my dear love,
And know that he, who loves you so,
From you shall my heart never go.
As long as I have breath, please know
The breeze of love will gently blow.

TO MY DEAR LOVE

I wish I was a red rose bush,
on the banks of the sea.
And every time my true love passed,
she would pluck a rose off of me!

I wish I was a water lily
floating on a pond so clear
and every time my true love passed
she would whisper something dear.

I wish I was a mountain so high,
glistening with pure white snow,
and every time my true love passed
I would melt and into a river flow.

I wish I was the God Mercury
descending from the sky,
and every time my true loved passed
with her I would gently lie.

WHEN I COME HOME TO YOU

When I come home to you
I'm going take you in my arms
And I'm gonna hold you tight.

LOVE: FROM THE DARKNESS TO THE LIGHT

When I set my loving eyes on you
I won't let you outta my sight.

When I come home to you
I'll kiss those sweet lips,
And know you are mine.
Oh baby you and I
Are gonna make love so fine.

When I come home to you,
Everything is gonna be alright
The clouds will disappear,
Because sweet baby of mine
To me you are so very dear.

When I come home to you,
The wind will never blow;
The sun will shine so bright
And in my living arms you
Will know everything is alright.

EMBRACING AN ANGEL

Please smile, dearest angel,
The pain you bare is not
As bad as you think
Because it is transitory.
To have such a scurrilous
Blight upon an angel
Would be an insanity.
You are serenely divine,
And as strikingly beautiful
As a crimson sunset
Over the mountains of time.
Your soul burns brightly, so
Never forget that my sweet girl.

LOVE: FROM THE DARKNESS TO THE LIGHT

> And never let temporary darkness
> Blind you from the glory that
> Waits to embrace an angel.

I hope you have enjoyed our journey from hopelessness into hope, our trip from being lost to being found, our sojourn from tears of misery to tears of joy. I am not a young man, so to find love in the later stages of my life is indeed gratifying. Modern technology allows love to flower across great distances, and I believe it is an improvement over the old way of finding love, because it allows people to explore compatibility in a somewhat anonymous fashion until they meet and then can spend time exploring the elements that bring love to life and make it either grow or prosper or wilt and die.

In the Tagalog language, the phrase "Mahal Kita" means "I love you." So I know share a poem that goes to the heart of love.

MAHAL KITA

> My darling, what I occasionally give you
> In the little pocket of hope called time
> I know brings you great joy.
> But it is small recompense
> For the love you show me.
> I cry tears of happiness when I see you smile,
> For you are the beating of my heart
> That was resurrected from the dark.
> You give your hand so sweetly.
> I am lost when you are away.
> You have me so completely.
> I cherish you night and day.
> Without your breath I cannot live.
> I need your lips on mine,

LOVE: FROM THE DARKNESS TO THE LIGHT

As I look into your eyes so divine.
In your arms I'm always home,
So happy and so proud to call you mine.
Never a day do I feel alone.
To the entire world I want to shout
Mahal Kita – Mahal Kita all about.

LOVE: FROM THE DARKNESS TO THE LIGHT

PART 3 – THE FRIVOLITY CAUSED BY THAT WHICH WAS FOSTERED FROM THE MOTIVATION PROVIDED BY MY MUSE

This was my most productive year as a writer. I finished six books in 10 months, doing one in less than 24 hours to match my hero, Mickey Spillane's feat of doing the same back in 1950. However, his 24 hour book sold over six million copies and mine will fall far short of that.

I attribute this incredible productivity to my beautiful muse, Lynton Viñas, who not only motivated me with her encouragement, but with her remarkable drive, desire and determination, as she works 12 hours a day six days a week. She is a human dynamo who never slows down, and never gives in to adversity. Put a roadblock before her, and she will figure out a way to go under, over or around it in some way.

The following material is either original poems or excerpts from some of the six books I produced during this remarkable year where I found time to relax in enchanting pleasure in a little love nest with the most incredible woman I have ever met, make love with regularity and write with a fury that often rivalled the speed of a Formula 1 racer heading toward the chequered flag. You will find them far reaching, but most with a centralized theme that offers an analysis of the human spirit and its potential in a world where greed rules supreme and too often imprisons people in service to an elite that does not know the meaning of compassion.

I proudly start off with a poem about my father, Worth Frye, whose biography I wrote in 2009 (2nd edition published in 2012). He was a man who probably crammed the equivalent of 5 or 6 lifetimes into 77 years and left a

LOVE: FROM THE DARKNESS TO THE LIGHT

lasting legacy that is still talked about throughout the southern United States, where he roared though life like a comet blazing through the midnight sky.

THE BALLAD OF JAMES WORTH FRYE

He roared out of a place called Farmer
Like a comet blazing through the midnight sky
Headed for the sweet bye and bye.
Listen now to the ballad of James Worth Frye.

When a huffing locomotive would come roaring by,
Crowds would holler "it's got as much steam as Frye."
Called a dare devil and hell in motion by all,
Some thought the man would one day fall.

Fear was not part of his game.
'Fore long, his bravery got him fame.
Like old Robert Mitchum in *Thunder Road*,
Worth hauled moonshine as his load.

He roared through Harlan County the devil at his tail,
"Damn that boy," said Sheriff Bobby McPhail.
He would shoot the gap at Cumberland
Barely even revving up his mill.

The feds threatened to close his door
With a bold warning in 1954.
Said "we got the roads covered now,
We're gonna get you – that's our vow."

Laughing it off with a sneer,
Worth sailed off without a care.
Like old Mitchum, he roared
Down the road in his '51 Ford.

LOVE: FROM THE DARKNESS TO THE LIGHT

The story is often told of what transpired.
Because of steel and iron Worth was sired.
"Ain't no fed gonna keep me from my chore.
Hell, they'll make me famous in folklore."

With G-men on his tail lights.
He knew there were road blocks up ahead.
"Hell" he said, "if I have to bend to the feds,
This old country boy had rather be dead."

Two patrol cars blocked the road,
But Worth was determined to deliver his load.
Slamming the pedal to the metal as bullets whizzed,
The feds tempers must have fizzed.

Worth blasted through the road block all hot,
Laughing at the feds and their silly lot.
He delivered his load in Ohio on time,
Cause he didn't see moon-shining as no crime.

He roared out of a place called Farmer
Like a comet blazing through the midnight sky
Headed for the sweet bye and bye.
Now you heard the ballad of James Worth Frye.

I had many heroes as a child and adolescent, but the two who stand out most were probably diametrically different when it came to capitalism. My dad was my hero, and he was a staunch capitalist. Of course, most of his younger life, capitalism was more pure until it was handed over to corporations by Ronald Reagan, who took office in 1981. My father and I had many lively political discussions, which often resulted in him calling me a communist, because I believed that an economic system based on greed was inherently evil. Like most young radicals, I had no room for compromise and could only see things my way.

LOVE: FROM THE DARKNESS TO THE LIGHT

Ironically, toward the end of his life, he moderated his views when he realized that free enterprise had been destroyed by corporations that exercise their enormous power to drive out competition and make the little guy unable to compete due to economies of scale.

My other hero was Che Guevara, who gave up a life of privilege as a physician to fight for the marginalized of the world. When asked why he became a revolutionary, he said, "I could have continued to be a physician and helped a few thousand people, or I could become a revolutionary and help millions. The choice was easy."

One book I wrote, entitled CHABLIS AND THE TERRORIST WHO RESURRECTED THE SPIRIT OF CHE GUEVARA, deals with the promise and hope that abounded when this remarkable individual walked the earth.

CHE GUEVARA LIVES

His name is a whisper on the wind.
Yes, listen to the whisper on the wind.
Che Guevara is more memory than man.
He never bowed in supplication to the mighty.
Wild eyed and fiery with passion he stood tall,
Fighting bravely to make the arrogant fall.
A legend that lives in the hearts and minds
Of all who long for freedom and justice,
Idealism eventually cost him his life.
But today, those who face poverty's strife
Can hear that whisper, that whisper on the wind.
"Che lives. Che Lives. Che lives.

JUSTICE AND HOPE LAID LOW

Hope was slain by the CIA in Bolivia

LOVE: FROM THE DARKNESS TO THE LIGHT

But Che's spirit still rides high and free.
Yes, this man was the Jesus of the modern age,
Crucified with a bullet fired from Washington.
The tiger was murdered by the worms
To protect the status-quo.
When they put him in an unmarked grave
Justice and hope were laid low.

ARCHITECT OF HIS OWN DESTINY

The merit of Marx is
that he suddenly produces a qualitative change
in the history of social thought.
He interprets history, understands its dynamic,
predicts the future, but in addition to predicting it,
he expresses a revolutionary concept:
the world must not only be interpreted,
it must be transformed,
So that man ceases to be the slave
and tool of his environment
and converts himself into
the architect of his own destiny.

PASS THE TORCH

Wherever death may surprise us,
let it be welcome,
provided that this our battle cry
may have reached some receptive ear
and another hand may be extended
to wield our weapons of revolution.

THE DISEASE OF GREED

How terrible is the pain of the mind and heart
When freedom is so unceremoniously suppressed.

LOVE: FROM THE DARKNESS TO THE LIGHT

Those who wallow in the misery of poverty
Are the most oppressed people of America.
The price they pay every day is a result
Of a system where those with the least
Are looked upon as malignant cancers
And discarded with contemptuous disregard
By a society that is itself diseased with greed.

JOHNNY PAYCHECK RIDES AGAIN

Johnny Paycheck Rides Again
Take this job and shove it
I ain't workin' here no more
I'm tired of working for no reward.
I can't even afford a used Ford.
I wonder what I'm working for.
Watch me walk out that door.

You better not try to stand in my way,
Cause I only got one thing to say.
I do all the work while you sit and read.
Just cause your uncle got you the job,
They pay you so much more.
Yeah, I'm walking out that door.

Been working here now for five long years,
Every day I go home and drown myself in tears.
Lots of good folks just like me are slaving away,
But others get the rewards at the end of the day.
And all I have is more bills piling high.
Hell, they even charge you when you die!

I've been waiting to get the guts to say:
Take this job and shove it.
I ain't working here no more.
Mess with me man and I'll have a fit

LOVE: FROM THE DARKNESS TO THE LIGHT

Take this job and shove it.
I ain't working her no more.
The bosses get their jobs by nepotism,
But each and everyone is a goddamn fool.
They prance around with noses in the air.
They think they are so damn cool.
I'll look at 'um and say, "Take this job and shove it.
I ain't working here no more."

While the privileged class plays golf, sits on their yachts sipping martinis, relaxes in their private jets on the way to the Riviera, or dines on caviar at their gated estates, those who toil in obscurity are ignored as nothing but the oil that greases the machinery of capitalism that chews them up. In the book CHABLIS AND THE TERRORIST WHO RESURRECTED THE SPIRIT OF CHE GUEVARA, one man begins a reign of terror aimed at corporate executives, and vows to exact justice against those who think they are above the law. The below excerpts are an example of how one determined individual can tackle the high and mighty and wreck havoc.

THE CHE GUEVARA MANIFESTO

Let all men and women of America know that the spirit of Che Guevara has been resurrected and justice is about to be meted out to the 1% who have gorged at the table of plenty far too long while disregarding the plight of those at the bottom of the economic ladder. The people at the bottom have been ignored by an uncaring government and beaten down for so long that they have lost the will to fight and demand justice. They now accept their fate as the government serves the interests of those at the top while ignoring the people who beg for a crumb from the table of plenty. I, the risen spirit of Che Guevara will rectify this by doing the following:

LOVE: FROM THE DARKNESS TO THE LIGHT

1. Be warned tyrants of commerce who accumulate wealth without sharing it with those who toil in despair for you. Your ruthless disregard for decency and fairness has been duly noted. Your worship at the altar of greed will finally make you reap what you have sown. Your day of reckoning is at hand. You will not be safe in your luxuriously appointed office. You will not be secure in your splendorous mansion in a guarded and gated community. You will not be immune from my wrath, although you are protected by bodyguards. Wherever you go or whatever you do always look over your shoulder, because retribution and divine vengeance for your misdeeds are close behind you. When you least expect it, the angel of retribution will appear with the sharp sword of vengeance to cut out the heart of evil that beats within your breast. Be aware that I shall not halt the punishment for your misdeeds with just you, because like the Bolsheviks who slew the Czar's family, I see the need to wipe out your evil seed; otherwise, your evil will be maintained in perpetuity through nepotism that assures your progeny will continue your despotic economic chicanery.

2. To those who treat employees with dignity, and share your bounty graciously, I say to you that no harm shall befall you from the spirit of Che. You know who you are, and I wish you to sleep well knowing that you are doing the right thing and shall be justly rewarded with continued life for you and your loved ones. However, be it proclaimed that the day will come when all will equally share in the bounty of this nation, so be prepared to give up your luxury, too, because as long as one man hungers, no man is entitled to accumulate too much. Until all have

shelter, sustenance, healthcare and any other necessity for a good and fruitful life no one should accumulate more than they need. You, too, must prepare for the day when all men and women in this nation will truly be free and equal. There will always be adequate room for the especially talented at the top, but you shall not be afforded exalted status, not allowed to store up excess at the expense of others.

3. Now, for those elected representatives who use their positions to serve the privileged, be forewarned, though the captains of industry are to be brought before the bar of my justice first, you are also on my list. Start now to do what you were elected to do and you may escape my wrath. Continue to put money in the pockets of weapons makers to prosecute wars of conquest all across the globe while ignoring the hungry, the sick, the homeless and the persecuted in this nation, and you, too, shall reap what you sow. Put an end to your excessive salaries, lavish retirement and parsimonious benefits. Close the revolving door between government and business, pass tax laws that are equitable by making the rich pay their fair share and you may escape my wrath; otherwise, you, too, should always be looking over your shoulders for the avenging angel.

4. To church leaders who support war and sanction the aggrandizement of greed, I say that you, too, must be vigilant. Do not use God to accumulate wealth for yourself and the hierarchy that runs religion. Use the money to lift up, not tear down. Avoid finger pointing as you remember what Jesus said, "Let he who is without sin cast the first stone." I shall give you time to make the necessary adjustments to rectify your drift into sanctifying the culture of greed and

justifying poverty, war and a host of abominations that you perpetrate in the name of God. I have no religion, but that does not make me unholy. I see suffering and try to heal it. I see war and try to stop it, and I see evil and confront it. It is your duty, as sworn servants of the one you call "the Prince of Peace" to do the same. See that you do, or you will also face the wrath of the avenging angel of justice.

5. I regret that things have gotten to point that these actions must be taken, but a nation that decries torture while it practices torture, a nation that preaches equality while promoting inequality,

A nation that calls itself god-fearing while committing acts of barbarity must be made to look within and see its own darkness. Hypocrisy was built into America from the start when its founders put in the phrase that all men were created equal while all but one of them were slaveholders. I say to all Americans that until you confront the hypocrisy and lies that enslave you this nation is doomed.

These are not idle threats that I am making, as by now you are aware of the execution of Thomas Kimberline. He is a relatively minor irritant in the grand scheme of things, but he is only the first of many who will fall. I am giving the CEO's of America two weeks to change things by asserting their intentions to do the right thing.

Be it further understood that I am exacting revenge for all the wrongs suffered by the downtrodden, those oppressed by a cruel, inhuman economic system that enslaves the many to the few. Revenge is an act of passion, and sometimes vengeance is the only avenue of justice available to the powerless. I am revenging injuries that have gone untreated for far too long. Be warned and be prepared, for the swift sword of justice is about to swing a mighty blow against oppression. Remember that justice cannot be for one side alone, but for all sides.

Sincerely, The Spirit of Che Guevara

REVENGE AND CRUELTY

Love has its place, as does hate.
Peace has its place, as does war.
Mercy has its place, as do cruelty and revenge.

The Spirit of Che Responds to the President's Lies

I, the spirit of Che Guevara, must respond to the lies of the President, because Americans swallow lies as if they were coming from the fountain of truth. But the fact is, in America, lies are substituted for the truth and the populace willingly swallows them because they have been propagandized into believing America is exceptional. Lies are part and parcel of what keeps those in power from ever really answering to the people. The people are so engrained with fear that they are easily manipulated into thinking the entire world is out to get the USA. The truth is the entire world just wants the USA to leave it alone. America has nothing most nations want. The freedom Americans enjoy is illusionary. How much freedom do you have when you can die because a cruel system based on greed that turns healthcare over to corporate executives who make decisions based upon the bottom line, not on compassion. Most civilized nations offer their citizens free and universal healthcare, but in a nation that aggrandizes greed, you are own your own when you get sick. The greatest disease in America is the disease of greed which afflicts every man, woman and child with its evil. How much freedom do you have when you can be locked up for checking out library books that the government deems subversive material? How much freedom do you have when the streets are filled with people carrying automatic weapons that can be bought easier than you can buy birth control pills? How much freedom do you have when corporations use your labour and then when you age dispose of you as a useless commodity and provide you with no decent pension for all you years of service? How much freedom do you have when due to the colour of your skin you are automatically assumed guilty and often executed on the spot by an overzealous police force that is there to protect the privileged class? How much freedom do you have when the sons and daughters of the poor are dispatched to fight wars of conquest while the sons and daughters of the privileged stay at home and enjoy their luxurious lifestyles in peace and splendour knowing they get all the benefits and never have to make any of the sacrifices?

Once again Mr. President, you have lied to the American people and they lap it up like someone who has gone without water for a week. They believe your lies, because inside they know the truth, and they do not want to face it. They do not want to face the reality of the shallowness of this nation when it comes to fair treatment. They live an illusion that is promulgated by a government that is there to serve the interests of the few at the expense of the many. That is the truth!

I say to you, Mr. President that the reason I fight is that I have compassion for those who do not have the will to fight for themselves. Most people in this nation have given up on changing things. I do not blame them, because they have been weakened by years of watching all the good things flow to those at the top. The children of the rich are exalted and given a preferred place at the table of plenty, and vetted with doors that open wide for opportunity, while the

LOVE: FROM THE DARKNESS TO THE LIGHT

government cuts funds for the poor to get educated while building more prisons than universities to house those who now are cash cows for the corporations that have taken over the incarceration business. This nation sees more corporate economic benefit to locking people up than educating them.

Your words define me as a terrorist, but rather, it is the corporation that is the true terrorist. It is the corporation, which is the holy grail of the wealthy, which brings people to their knees in supplication to the will of a monolithic monster. There is no core to this nation. Its heart has been ripped out and sacrificed at the altar of greed. There is no moral fibre left, as capitalism is even promoted as the preferred choice of Jesus, who, in reality, was the world's greatest socialist who told the rich man – give all you have to the poor. I, like he was, am a social reformer. I am taking up arms against the greatest oppressor of mankind – the corporation which represents the interests of the rich and keeps my brothers and sisters chained in misery and ignominy. I take up arms in response to the oppressor, and if the people begin to free themselves from propaganda, they will join me in tumbling this hypocrisy that keeps them in chains, and it is the thought of an aroused, fed-up public that you fear most. For once the people see what real freedom is like; there will be no stopping them. For he who has tasted true freedom has eaten the earth's most bountiful harvest.

Sincerely,

The Spirit of Che Guevara

OUR DAILY BREAD

The seeds of revolution
are not planted by one person,

LOVE: FROM THE DARKNESS TO THE LIGHT

but by the misery of those
who toil in obscurity
for their daily bread.

I AWAIT THE REVOLUTION

In a world of despair and misery
The rich turn a blind eye to poverty.
They disregard those at the bottom
Of each society's economic ladder
While worshipping the God of money,
Laughing at inequality as if it was funny.

Politicians line up to gorge themselves
At the corporate trough of bribery,
Selling themselves to the highest bidder,
While ignoring those who toil for a penance
Just to keep food on their table,
While rich women prance in coats of sable.

Thou shalt not kill is a commandment
In that book that so many revere.
Do these people not realize that by allowing
The hoarding of wealth they are killing?
The God they worship provided manna for all
If it is shared according to Jesus' clarion call.

The admonition to not kill
Should apply to a world economy
Based on exclusion and inequality,
Because such a system murders hope.
The rich do not pray – they prey
On those who have been denied any say.

The trickle-down theory is encouraged
As a panacea by those at the top.

LOVE: FROM THE DARKNESS TO THE LIGHT

"Just give us more and some will flow to you"
Is the cry of those on Wall Street.
Alas, little is left when those at the top
Gorge themselves and cannot stop.

When the stock market crashes or even loses a point,
It is news of grave concern by those who rule.
Yet, when a homeless person dies from hunger or exposure,
It is that person's fault for not working hard enough.
The world today is obsessed with greed,
But those at the top are sowing a deadly seed.

The call for free markets that will bring
About greater justice and end inequality
Is a magician's trick of smoke and mirrors
Perpetrated by those who have control of the markets.
They demand a crude naïve trust from those they chain
But, oh, those at the top wear the mark of Cain.

As Cain slew his brother Abel, these cretins
Slay hope and promise for the poor
Who must toil in obscurity for their daily bread.
Oh holy lie, unfettered capitalism destroys more than it saves,
Making those at the bottom suffer an ill fate.
It is a glorious revolution of the poor for which I await!

HOPE

Though the mills of hope grind slowly:
They still grind ever so methodically.
Fate stands anticipatorily waiting,
As with exactness it grinds all.

> Greed is the elixir of the devil.

LOVE: FROM THE DARKNESS TO THE LIGHT

JUSTICE

I am the Shadow that stalks the night!
I am the scourge of the arrogant, self-indulgent shallow
who rule with the iron fist of repression.
Where there is injustice,
I will be there lurking in the shadows to strike.
The government is there to protect the chosen few...
those that would prey on the innocent.
I will right the wrongs and bring justice or die trying.

THE EVIL OF GREED

I hunger for a dish of vengeance
With gravy made of the wealthy's blood.
I want a dessert of glorious retribution.
I long for a repast of sweet revenge
That is icy cold around the edges
And as hot as molten lead at the core.

Let me make medicine of great revenge
To cure this intense deadly grief that has
Been hoisted by those who sit in splendour
Dining on the fatted calf while the rest of us
Scramble for the crumbs that dribble from
The table of plenty in the hall of disregard.

I shall not depend on God to cure the ills
Of economic discontent that abound,
For he has done a less than credible job
In the proper dispensation of the wealth
That should be shared rather than hoarded.
Therefore, my gun is ready and the trigger cocked.

We live on an earth where the goddess of wealth
Is worshipped as if gold was in her hair.

LOVE: FROM THE DARKNESS TO THE LIGHT

Her smile lures those who long for riches.
People drink the very diamond of her air.
Her breath perfumed silver for the while,
All sanctity and fairness do defile.

And wake for her the gifted line,
That wild and witchingly lay,
And swear all hearts are her shrine,
That only owns her greed induced sway.
That I swear to seek revenge at last
Marked by that scornful cheek I turn.

Ay, now by all the bitter tears
That I have shed for the poor,
The racking doubts, the burning fears,
Avenged they well may be.
The days of endless woe
Caused by the rich who are our foe.

I wish to see these barons of greed laid
Within a dastardly cold tomb,
For they all humanity have betrayed,
And only brought on their own doom.
It is I who will provide fitting punishment and pain.
My sweet revenge for the afflicted who toil in vain.

Go thou and watch their lightest sigh,
And bark discontent beneath her greedy eye.
I shall not turn on thee who in poverty lie,
For I, the spirit of Che, will deliver the blow
That will provide sweet retribution
and lay the evil of greed low.

Writing a book (LYNTON AND THE VAMPIRE AT TAGAYTAY MANOR) about three heroic women pursuing

LOVE: FROM THE DARKNESS TO THE LIGHT

a vampire, the following describes Ambrogio, the very epitome of evil.

In the place called Taal Heritage Village near the town of Tagaytay in the Philippines, evil lurks in the form of Ambrogio, as he pursues one of the heroines in an attempt to "turn her" into a creature of the night. Only the love of her two friends saves her.

FRIGHT NIGHT AT THE TAAL HOTEL

Once upon a Poe midnight dreary,
while she pondered weak and weary,
suddenly there came a tapping from behind,
some one gently rapping, rapping at her sombre mind.
Could it be someone with malevolent intent?
It was such a black night,
And there was a ghostly presence in the shadows
as vainly she had sought to borrow sanity.
She was lamenting her lost love
who had left her when push came to shove.

And the uncertain rumbling of the volcano's curtain
filled her with fantastic terrors never felt before.
She stood still, hearing the beating of her heart.
Who is this visitor of the mind?
Can it be a demon unkind?

"Sir," she shouted and turned.
The slight rapping of a cane stopped.
She stood in silence staring into the blackness.
The shadows danced in the darkness with despair.
She stood there this lady so fair.

Deep into that darkness peering,
She was still quiet and fearing.

LOVE: FROM THE DARKNESS TO THE LIGHT

Doubting, dreaming dreams of demons in the dark..
But the silence was unbroken,
and the darkness gave her no token.
Back toward the volcano turning,
all her soul began burning,
Soon again she heard a tapping louder than before.
"Surely," said she, "surely there is something there.
Can it be a demon from fanciful lore?"

Suddenly emerging from the darkness with a flutter,
yes, it was like the flutter of a bat's wings,
stood tall, ram-rod straight Lekman Lopez,
his eyes honed in on her and he says,
"Listen to the volcano as a sweet melody it sings."

Seemingly extreme obeisance made he;
but not a minute stopped or tarried he;
but, with mien of lord on high,
perched above Ingrid he moved forward
and she swooned as in his arms she wanted to lie.

There was not any need for smiling,
as in his cold red eyes she saw the grave.
He swept her into his arms as he was craven.
His sharp teeth glistened in the moonlight.
How he desired the neck of the sweet young maiden.
Lekman Lopez whispered softly,
"Relax as it will not hurt.
Listen to the lonely, sorrowful rumble of Taal.
Ah, its sweet sorrow is music to my ears.
After my bite you shall have no fears."

His soul in those words he did outpour.
Nothing further did he utter,
but Ingrid heard a light flutter,
as his black cloak flapped in the breeze,

LOVE: FROM THE DARKNESS TO THE LIGHT

and she fell into his arms with ease.
Startled at the stillness as no words were aptly spoken,
she was hypnotically willing to court disaster
in the arms of he who was now her master.
Ill-will for blood, he so proudly bore
for he had long ago closed heaven's door.

Lekman Lopez was most beguiling,
his sad soul was smiling.
Into his arms Ingrid was slowly sinking,
but he desired blood from this sweet miss,
sighing in ecstasy waiting for the kiss.

So enthralled, she did not engage in guessing,
for no syllable was expressing.
This bat of a man whose fiery eyes now burned
into her wilting soul's core;
lust for blood was what he had learned.

Then, the air grew denser,
perfumed from an unseen censor.
Swung by from heaven, two angels appeared.
"Evil wretch," cried Lynton.
"Deplorable heathen," shouted Channa.

Lekman turned from his prey,
his eyes burning with hate.
Smiling, he whispered his evil.
"No one can avoid their fate.
Time will come when you rue this day".

"Thing of evil," said Lynton.
Channa, her precise diction not wavering, cried,
"Your evil we will bury where you lie."
Disconsolate, yet completely undaunted,
Lekman with words the women assaulted.

LOVE: FROM THE DARKNESS TO THE LIGHT

"I have wandered this earth for thousands of years.
People like you cause the children of the night no fears.
Even heaven bends before me.
No one will believe what you say
you have seen on this dark day."

"Demon!" said Lynton, "thing of evil!"
"This is a woman we adore.
From her, there shall be no blood.
We have defeated demons before.
We know how to close the devil's door."

Lekman, his eyes like smouldering embers, said
"Be careful my beauties when you mess with the un-dead.
You are fair and radiant maidens
but you are no match for me.
Just wait. Just wait and you will see."

"Be that word our sign of parting fiend!' shrieked Lynton
"Get thee back into hell from whence you came.
We place no credence in the lies you have spoken!
Leave us and our souls will stay unbroken!
We seek solace not glory or fame."
And Lekman, never flitting,
still was smiling, yes still smiling,
as if dreaming a demon's dream
sitting by the devil's stream
plotting about their defiling.

The moonlight throws his shadow on the ground,
and these girls souls are easily found.
He turns to walk away as they embrace,
As together they know any evil they can face.
Then the volcano makes that loathsome sound.

In an instance they hear the flutter of wings.

LOVE: FROM THE DARKNESS TO THE LIGHT

They look skyward at the full moon hanging high,
and there fluttering across it eerily in the sky
is a giant bat whose image blackens the night
and fills all who gaze upon it with fright.

THE GHOST

Just like an angel with evil eye,
I shall return to thee silently,
Upon thy bower I'll alight,
With falling shadows of the night

With thee, the dead, I'll commune,
And give thee kisses cold as the moon,
And with a serpent's moist embrace,
I'll crawl around thy resting-place.

And when the livid morning falls,
You will find alone the empty walls,
And till the evening, cold 'twill be.

As others with their tenderness,
Upon thy life and youthfulness,
I'll reign alone with dread o'er thee.

FEAR THAT WHICH WANTS YOUR TRUST

America, which was founded by revolution,
Has great fear of revolution.
The government uses fear to keep the populace in bondage.
The government fears the people might wise-up
and demand fairness,
and that is why there must be a scapegoat,
whether it is a Muslim chopping someone's head off
in a far-away land or a person of colour living
in the ghetto who wants a welfare check.

LOVE: FROM THE DARKNESS TO THE LIGHT

America building more prisons than universities
and allowing the barbarity of torture
to fight terrorism is permissible and just.
Welfare to corporations and the rich in the form
of an unfair tax structure is just good economics
according to the American government.
So, fear is the enemy of justice
But Americans should know what
They should fear most is their own government.

HER EVIL BITES AND CLEAVES

Her evil bites and cleaves so tight,
Even when you think she has moved on.
She dropped a pebble in the water:
Just a splash, and it was gone;
But there are now a million ripples
circling on and on and on,
Spreading, spreading from the centre,
Flowing out to the turbulent sea.
And there is no way of telling
Where the end will finally be.

Her evil bites and cleaves so tight,
Even when you think it has moved on.
Dropped a pebble in the water, and from
That ripple a great big wave has grown;
She disturbed a peaceful stream
Just by dropping in a little stone.
On and on the evil did slowly grow
As the tiny ripple is on the go,
And there is no way to stop ripples,
Once you've started them to flow.

Her evil bites and cleaves so tight,
Even when you think it has moved on.

LOVE: FROM THE DARKNESS TO THE LIGHT

Drop an insignificant stone in carelessness,
Commit an act that seems benign,
But there's little waves a-flowing,
And there's ripples circling yet.
And now her evil in some sad heart
A mighty wave of tears has stirred,
And disturbed a life that was happy
With a ripple from the devil's word.

Her evil bites and cleaves so tight,
Even when you think it has moved on.
The evil was in response to kindness.
Just a flash of hatred and it is gone;
But there's a million ripples now
circling on and on and on,
Destroying hope, joy and comfort
On each splashing, dashing wave
Until you couldn't believe the volume
From one stone that now has made love's grave.

THROUGH THE VEIL OF TEARS

I heard the news of his death
at a time when I felt dead myself.
I was in the army involved in
another immoral and unjust war.
His death made me realize that
I had to live every minute with
the realization that none of us
knows when the grim reaper might
swing his scythe as he gallops
astride the black horse of death.
Jimmy Grimsley was a friend,
and many times over the years
I have recalled his untimely demise.
How strange that someone who

LOVE: FROM THE DARKNESS TO THE LIGHT

has been gone for over 40 years,
can still have an effect on you
reaching through the veil of tears.

GINSBERGIAN METAPHORS OF OUTRAGE

Ginsbergian metaphors float on a crimsoned sky,
where dreams float about awhile and then die.

What hammer of iron bashed open their skulls
and ate up their brains and imagination?
Filth! Ugliness! Ash cans of unobtainable dollars!
Children screaming under the stairways!
The poor in armies of discontent weep in their misery.
Incomprehensible prisons built to house those
who dare question the economic order of things.
The system causes a congress of sorrows.
The God these people are to worship is green.
Money is the cannibal that devours all.
Skyscrapers erected to greed stand like sphinxes
over the streets that are but smoking tombs.
The air belches fogs of greed from those
who cannot see anything but dollars signs.
Poverty dances among the spectre of genius,
Light streaming out of the smog filled sky!
Robot apartments! Invisible suburbs!
Skeleton treasuries! Blind capitalists!
Demonic industries! Spectral nations! A madhouse!
Build monstrous bombs to subdue
while ignoring hunger in the mist.
They break their backs lifting caches of money for
those who rain like royalty over all.
Malls, movies and televisions to occupy time
so that rebellion will be stayed.
Orwellian slavery is the destiny of all.
Visions! Omens! Hallucinations! Miracles! Ecstasies!

LOVE: FROM THE DARKNESS TO THE LIGHT

gone down the river of no return.
Dreams! Adorations! Illuminations! Hope!
Awaits in the arms of Jesus who
is used by the wealthy to placate
those who want heaven now.
Wait! Wait! Wait! Wait!
The hereafter will reward you with some gold.
They see it all, but are given none.
Capitalism blots out the hopeful sun.

Ginsbergian metaphors float on a crimsoned sky,
where dreams float about awhile and then die.

TO MY FRIEND CHRISTINE

It is true that birds of a feather
Really do stick together.
Which is why I'll never regret,
That fateful day when we met.
Oh, how grateful I am to Skype.
It brought us together in celestial light.
Thank you for being a good friend.
I'll stick with you until the end!

Love can be shared not just between two humans, but between human and animal. Sometimes that is the purest form of love. I witnessed that kind of love between my ex-wife and her cat, Tito. These following two poems glorify that perfect love between them.

TITO'S GRAVE

Here, in her soft heart
Where roses once bloomed,
Where laurel and vine mingled,
Where the turtledove cooed,

LOVE: FROM THE DARKNESS TO THE LIGHT

Where the cricket sang in delight,
What grave is this that lies in sight?
Adorned by a man who observed you two
With a stone bearing his name.
With loving beauty he is at rest.
Ah, he enjoyed winter and spring
Resting in your warm arms.
This was your true love,
And you shelter him still
Deep within your beating heart.
No man will ever capture your soul
As he who lies in the ground cold.
Tito the Cat from your heart will never depart.

WHEN JASMINE MEETS TETE
IN THE SWEET BYE AND BYE

I spent the day with Jasmine
who harmoniously compliments the sun.
I was reminded as I looked over at her
of the day she stood by a grave
with tears cascading down her cheeks,
telling me to adjust her dead cat's tail.
"He doesn't like it that way," she said.
My heart ached for what she had lost.
Her pain was my pain for sure,
as my love was so true and pure.

Just this side of forever is a place called love.
Tito was a cat who touched her heart.
But he now frolics through meadows
and up lovely little grass-laden hills
in a place where there is plenty of water,
food and sunshine to make him comfortable.
In this magnificent place he is restored
to absolute perfect health and vigour.

LOVE: FROM THE DARKNESS TO THE LIGHT

He is free of the disease that laid him low.
Yet, he longs for she who did not want to let him go.

Tito is content in this place of mirth,
except that he misses she who was so special.
As he plays for years and years, he still waits
at the top of the hill each day for she whom he misses.
40 years after his death, he bounds to the hilltop.
He suddenly stops and stares into the distance.
His bright eyes are beams if intensity.
His eager body quivers and quakes.
He springs down the hill flying over the grass.
What he sees coming is his past.

There she is, not an old woman, but young
as she was when he left her long ago.
She runs toward him with tears of joy.
Bending down, she embraces him
and whispers in a soft, melodious voice:
"We will never part again, I promise."
Happy kisses are planted on his face,
her hand caresses his beloved furry head.
She looks into the trusting eyes of he who left long ago.
And from her that old wonderful love will flow.

ROAR FOR EVERMORE

He loved the rumbling of the engine
and the sweet sigh of shifting gears.
This was a real trucking man
barrelling through the promised land.

He has delivered his last load,
and earned his eternal rest,
for now he is driving where
they know he did his best.

LOVE: FROM THE DARKNESS TO THE LIGHT

He was a brave knight of the road,
devoted and true to the trucker's code.
When he drives to heaven's pearly gate,
St. Peter will say, "Roll on in mate."

His run is finally over,
But remember him forevermore,
All across the nation
as our 18 wheelers roar.

HOMAGE TO A WEEK OF BLISS

I remember the good times,
that father and daughter once had...
but still my life today,
is oh...so sad.

I try to look forward,
but my mind goes back...
because a piece of the glass,
on my life portrait is cracked.

I tried hard to protect the glass,
Not to let it founder and profoundly shatter...
Still it crashed, but my daughter,
now you are again a part of what matters.

I have never been great
or the "best father"...
And, at times I've failed
as so many times I falter.

For those things I am sorry,
I don't want you to cry...
but please remember,
but neither are my eyes dry.

LOVE: FROM THE DARKNESS TO THE LIGHT

I hope you know
that our love was never lost...
it was simmering with fate
for you to rescue me at any cost

My dear wife,
is missing and gone...
And everything feels,
Oh...so wrong

But, there you are with love.
That is what you can do...
I will try to be strong
and determined just for you.

One thing I feel
down deep in my heart...
It's my love for you
I guess that's a start.

You have a life of your own
but love for me is deep inside,
And, I hope that you know
that I look upon you with pride.

You have made me feel love
like I have never felt before.
It is you I have come to admire,
and to more completely adore.

It's a new beginning for us
based upon a most glorious past.
My pain is so intense,
but your love will not let it last.

When you reached out to me,

LOVE: FROM THE DARKNESS TO THE LIGHT

I sense that your affection is as solid as a rock fence,
as it reflects the knowledge of father
who taught you to love so intense.

You brought a ray of hope
the past few days to one who had lost his way.
You see, I now am old and it is I who
depend on you. I love you. What else can I say?

Meet Chablis Louise Chavez in the following passages. My muse, Lynton Vinas, and my friend Christine Sagrado were instrumental in motivating me to invent this character that was born into adversity but never gave in to despair. She is a light that shines brightly in the darkness.

HE NEVER FALTERED

Chablis turned to him and said, "Without communication there is no love, without respect there is no love, without trust there is no love. I have your respect. I have your love. I have your trust. I can see it in your eyes. I can feel it in my heart."

Looking back at Chablis with deep intensity, Aaron replied, "Chablis, I love you so much. Remember it is better to lose your pride with someone you love rather than to lose that someone you love with useless pride. Never fear coming to me, because I am here for you. I am prepared to do my penance by serving you and making your life all it can be. You are the light of my life, a beacon that shines in the darkness of my miserable existence. You can never be mine. I know that now, but it makes no difference, because I am a prisoner of love and cannot climb that wall of despair that traps me. All I can do is promise to never desert you, to always be the man of

LOVE: FROM THE DARKNESS TO THE LIGHT

whom you will one day say after I am gone that he never faltered in his devotion to me."

NOBODY IS PEREFCT

Chablis thought to herself: Never leave a relationship because of a few faults. Nobody is perfect, nobody is correct in the end. Sam was as close to perfect for her as any man she had ever known. He did not care about her anatomy. How many times had she heard him say, "I love you, not your anatomy?" For him, Chablis was the bright sun that came up over the horizon each day and serenely shined a light of contentment on a man who had been on a precipice of despair. She was hope, charity and promise.

AVENGING ANGEL FOR THE FORGOTTEN IN THE CITY OF LOST HOPE

Meanwhile, in Mai-Mai's opulently appointed apartment furnished, not by her riches, but by the riches of the men she used, the magnificence of what she thought was the good life was nothing more than shallowness of a soul that knew no restraint when it came to manipulation and the avarice pursuit of satisfaction that simply was forever elusive. The opulence of the life she lived represented illumination she thought, but it was actually a darkness that could not be reached by any light. Her possessions were all poor and worthless compared to the common light which the sun sends to the windows of people like Chablis who toil in obscurity. That light offered by people like Chablis pours over valley, hill and mountaintop kindling the sky of hope with reason, conscience and love. It offers a dignity of worth rather than the indignity of avaricious greed found in the lives of people like Mai-Mai. Chablis was a woman just the opposite of Mai-Mai. Chablis was the sweet avenging angel for the forgotten in the city of lost hope.

LOVE: FROM THE DARKNESS TO THE LIGHT

PURITY OF SOUL

Then, there was Chablis, who was the true saint in a world filled with demons. She was the avenging angel who stood by all who dared have hope in a world where hope was dashed in the pit of despair called capitalism. Chablis, a fortification against all who dared make war on the weakest among us, was not just a woman, she was the woman. The woman who refused to bend before prejudice, judgmental arrogance or the finger pointing hypocrites who wanted to trap all of humanity in obedience to a God of vengeance rather than a God of love. Hey, Chablis was love. Yes, her demure way, her captivating smile, her eyes shining with kindness, even her succulent lips that offered carnal delights were all part and parcel of she who knew no sin of conscience. Her conscience was as pure as the driven snow on a crisp brisk winter day in December. If purity could be bottled and sold, Chablis' purity would command top dollar.

CHABLIS' LEGS

Burroughs pointed to a chair, indicating that Chablis should take a seat. He pulled up a chair across from her and obviously enjoyed watching her cross her legs. Of course, Chablis was not above using everything in her arsenal of sex appeal to get what she wanted from men. Her long, cascading hair that flowed like a river of desire was frequently brushed back with her soft, dainty hands that all men wanted to feel stroking their bodies. Her dancing bedroom eyes were flush with sensuality. Her pouty, moist, succulent lips that seemed to beg for a kiss were purposely licked by her tongue that she let linger on them just a second so the observer could imagine what it would be like to have it plunge into the mouth and dart about. Oh, but her legs. Her toned, smooth legs glistened like fine silk and the

LOVE: FROM THE DARKNESS TO THE LIGHT

muscular calves flexed with just the right amount of tenseness that made men dream of having them wrapped around them as she could pulled them deep inside her, imprisoning a lover in their vice-like grip. Her legs were simply the greatest asset in her armoury of sexuality. They offered a reassured pleasurable treasury of delight, a brilliance that seemed to sparkle like a diamond.

Finally, a bit of erotica in regards to Chablis who is a free spirit when it comes to sex. Hey, it is my book let me have a little fun.

PROBE OF LOVE

Her cherub bottom was lovingly shaped,
So round and plump with exquisiteness.
Arched up, she met each thrust with glee,
Her passion like a raging storm at sea.

Between those soft pert cheeks,
Upon her fragile quivering soft skin,
rested his instrument of love,
as she longed for each shove.

The sweet nubile vixen Chablis
Saturated his soul and flooded his being.
She was a wanton, lustful delight,
Making his soul take flight.

Quietly she sighed an erotic tune.
She snaked and gyrated with pleasure.
As deep inside her went each thrust.
There was passion, ardour and lust.

Chablis was a Goddess of light.
She was a beacon of sexual thirst.

LOVE: FROM THE DARKNESS TO THE LIGHT

His explosion rattled her soul,
Writing satisfaction on passion's scroll

THE TICK TOCK OF LOVE

Tick tock, tick tock, tick tock go the hands of time
Moving inexorably toward the day of my demise.
The approach of eternity makes one reflect,
Because the grim reaper no one can deflect.
Life has been one of chasing a demon of the mind.
Oh, how I longed for blissful peace to find.

Three gems of worth made my spirit soar,
As if I was trapped in a great tale of lore.
She whom I loved left me all alone
Unloved, un-cherished and unknown.
My mind is in search of an open door
To a time when children beat at my golden core.

Remembering the air was filled with glee,
Those three gems played happily at my knee.
I tried so hard to tend them with loving care,
Fighting desperately to keep them from fear.
But now they have gone, each to their own life.
One to a husband and two to a wife.

I now sit alone wiping a golden tear,
But still in my heart they are near.
My time left here is oh so brief.
Still, I have no reason for grief.
I lovingly un-braid my children in the mind,
For they to a lonely father are never unkind.

They reflect soulfully on all the love to them I have shown,
And though distance keeps us apart I am not alone.
In my heart, they dwell in contemplative splendour so sure,

LOVE: FROM THE DARKNESS TO THE LIGHT

Knowing that between us is a love deep, abiding and pure.
Tic tock, tick tock, tick tock go the hands of time
As I smilingly await the apocalyptic horseman to ride.

Oh yes, the clock chimes my final journey to the dark,
But as I reach out to embrace the veil, I refuse to embark
Without one final cry into the wilderness of the loving past.
You see, I realize that after I am gone something will last.
I shall embrace them within my loving heart so sublime,
As the clock goes tick tock, tick tock, tick tock a last time.

MAKE A DIFFERENCE

Look all about and you see people
Who just settle for the normal.
These people fear rocking the boat of conventionality.
Do not be content with what is expected.
Be bold and forceful in pursuit of truth.
Tackle life instead of letting life tackle you.
Don't fear being the odd man out.
Be happy to eschew the monetary
for the sanctity of helping others.
Never look at the affluent as privileged.
They live in a world of opulence
but in reality are poor in spirit.

The truly wealthy are those who have independence
and value not the superficial but value values.
Cultivate relationships with those who offer
depth of character and will not put restraints
on your hopes, dreams and aspirations.
Know that reality should be revealed, not concealed.

Do not be beholding to government, corporations
churches or individuals that keep you in invisible chains.
Answer to no one but your inner voice of reason.

LOVE: FROM THE DARKNESS TO THE LIGHT

Believe in yourself not in someone
with questionable motives.
Do what is right not what is expedient.
Believe in principle over profit and love over hate.

Believe that expediency is trumped by wise planning.
Know the difference between owning things
and letting things own you.
Know that a person is not a commodity.
A person is a resource that cannot be bought and sold.
Therefore, do not put your soul on the auction block.

Believe in you and your promise.
Give your time, energy and support to a cause.
Innovate for the benefit of all, not the few.
That way you shall always serve the greater good.
When all is said and done don't just be different.
Make a difference.

THE SPIRIT OF COMPASSION

There should be a spirit about the land,
When the old idea of greed
Is buried deep in the sand.

It is time to think of what
We owe other men,
Not what we can get from them.

It is time people had the compassion
To not to fill their own bellies,
When others go hungry.

It is time for men to be unable
To sleep in a warm bed,
When others shiver in the cold.

LOVE: FROM THE DARKNESS TO THE LIGHT

It is time for the warmongers
To be stripped of their weapons
And men of peace to prevail.

It is time for the charlatans of religion
To be exposed for their hypocrisy
And the light of truth to shine.

There should be a spirit about the land,
When men of goodwill together band,
And the fires of hope are fanned.
Let the words of Che ring true.
"If you tremble with indignation at any injustice,
Then you are a comrade of mine."

THE NURSE

When my dear nurse looks at me
she sees a light of intensity,
not a cranky old man who is not very wise.
She does not see me
as one uncertain of habit
with staring glassy eyes
who dribbles his food and makes no reply.
She just softly whispers, "Please try."
She may think I don't recognize all she tries to do
when I don't even seem to know the difference
between a sock and a shoe.
She refuses to accept my dying will
as the long dreary days she tries to fill.
Unlike others, she opens her eyes
when she looks at me.
She lets me tell her who I am
with my eyes as I sit so still.
When I was young and had wings on my feet

LOVE: FROM THE DARKNESS TO THE LIGHT

I dreamed of a lover too soon meet.
That lover is now gone from me,
and eternity is there for me to see.
I am just an old man
who has learned nature is cruel.
The body crumbles – grace and vigour depart.
But I see love in my nurse's heart.
So, inside this carcass a young man dwells
as my battered heart soars and swells.
I remember the joys and the pain,
as she helps me live life again.
I realize things have gone too fast
and that nothing can last.
.But looking at my nurse when I fade away
will make everything seem peacefully O.K.

CHANGE

I changed my hair. I changed my style
I changed my look. I changed my smile.
I changed my clothes to suit the fad.
I changed the humble nature that I had.
I changed the way I walked and talked.
I changed my diet and my routine.
I even changed my fitness machine.
I changed my lifestyle.
I changed my ideals.
I changed my character.
I changed my friends.
I changed the way the story ends.
I changed the goals and sights I'd see.
I changed everything that made me - me.
I changed my overall direction.
I changed how I viewed my reflection.
Then, I realized I was not me anymore.
So, I changed back to the way I was before.

LOVE: FROM THE DARKNESS TO THE LIGHT

REFLECTIONS IN A MIRROR THAT ONCE LIED

Despite her physical birth defect,
she demanded respect.
When she was a child it became clearer.
She looked long and hard in the mirror
Gazing between her legs she knew it lied.
The boy in her immediately died.

People did not understand
Because she lived in a strange land.
What people wanted to see
Was dictated by the church's key
That unlocked a door to intolerance,
Making people show their ignorance.

As a youth she laughed and cried,
The intolerance she defied.
She wore silk and lace,
And had such a dainty face.
Slowly the mirror stopped its lie,
Her spirit of freedom decided to fly.

As a young woman filled with grace,
A man fell into her embrace.
He never saw the mirror lie,
Because convention he would never try.
Together the years rolled on.
He'd love her until he was gone.

This man in her arms swooned,
Their spirits in sink attuned.
He saw her for what she was,
Because his love never took pause.
He knew the mirror didn't really lie.
In it was a woman who made his spirits fly.

LOVE: FROM THE DARKNESS TO THE LIGHT

WHERE MONSTERS GROW

Beware of the monsters
Who dwell in the mind,
Who grow in the shelter
Of shadows they find.
Beware of the demons
Who hide from the light,
Who only survive
When hidden from sight.
These creatures can thrive
Where diligence is low;
They fill in the spaces
Of what we don't know.
Beware of the monsters
That are filled with hate,
They strike out in anger
When we can't relate.
Our own ignorance darkens
The mind and the heart,
And lets the monsters
Inside to tear us apart.
The witching hour is at hand.
At lonely Tagaytay Manor on high,
Lekman Lopez arises from his coffin
To flap his wings and fly.

PREGNANCY MAKES YOU BEAUTIFUL

I saw her coming toward me
With a swift and sure glow,
More beautiful than I remember
When I met her nearly a year ago.

In the SM Mall she moved gracefully
To greet me with a fond "hello"

LOVE: FROM THE DARKNESS TO THE LIGHT

From sweet her did a smile
Gently and progressively grow.

Her husband by her side was so proud.
A protrusion for four months had grown.
She was regal like a queen with child
Ready to sit on motherhood's throne.

Her radiant beauty showed happiness galore,
As her tummy held that which she would adore.
Now her loveliness is so easy to see
As that within makes her beauty soar.

SONG OF INGRID

There is peace in her soul.
A love of melody and rhyme
Once you look into her heart.

Take heed those who seek the pure of heart.
She is a woman of infinite charm,
Whose beauty and allure are legendary
In sounding passion's alarm.

You will know how deep within you have reached,
As whispered fate takes your hand offering love
you never dreamed would be breached.

Her name is Ingrid in a far off land,
Where hummingbirds sing her praise
And the nightingales hark of her beauty.

CHRISTINE! CHRISTINE! CHRISTINE!

Lies often pile up high.
On a bright and sunny day,

LOVE: FROM THE DARKNESS TO THE LIGHT

friends seem to abound,
but when the sky is blue
they can hardly be found.

Just wait for a raging storm,
when darkness overwhelms you,
when the days grow barren and cold,
and laughter is no longer heard,
and your heavy heart is no longer bold.

Then, a friend arrives from a land afar,
and stands lovingly beside you,
lifts your spirits to the sky,
and laughter returns with a fury,
as loneliness you now defy.

You are the bright sunshine
in a world of darkness.
Sweetness in you is easily seen.
In my heart I can only proclaim
Christine! Christine! Christine

REMEMBERING SHE WHO CARED

She has been gone for nearly 50 years now,
But before her unrestrained love I still bow.
I think about her each and every day,
And how I long for her when I cry.
So much has happened in my life,
As many odds I have had to defy.

I remember how I used to welcome her embrace,
When tough times I had to face.
And that sweet aroma would be intoxicating,
As the scent of snuff was on her breath,
The feel of love from within was exhilarating.

LOVE: FROM THE DARKNESS TO THE LIGHT

But like us all she was claimed by that demon death.
Though time has ticked on her image never fades,
As I recall for me she always had accolades.
She taught me to never give into adversity's knock,
When my heart was burdened with pain,
Because love from her made heaven's gate unlock,
And I knew there was much for me to gain.

The word grandmother rings a tone of hope,
Even though without her it is hard to cope.
The lives she touched with acts of kindness
Prove that she still sees and feels our tears,
Because we are all free of unjust blindness
That would keep us trapped in dark fears.

FATE COMES CALLING

Fate is a silent hunter
that perches in the dark.
On each individual
it leaves its mark.

It's calling when least expected
And may cut you in two.
Do you even know when
it is whispering to you?

Take it to the real world,
then break it in half.
Just roll life's dice
and that will suffice.

Sense it in your heart.
Don't take it for granted.
On a precipice you stand.
It will use you if it can.

LOVE: FROM THE DARKNESS TO THE LIGHT

When fate comes calling
what can you do?
When fate comes calling
what can you do?

STAND TRIUMPHANT

Remember that ultimately we all answer to ourselves
People may push you around.
People may say negative things.
People may point the finger of condemnation.
But do not bend before the winds of discontent.
Do not let stress, uncertainty or unkind words
Keep you from achieving your dreams.
Remain confident, focused and true to yourself,
And in the end, you will stand triumphant.

I want to end this book with a bit of frivolity, so lets try the following and see if it puts a smile on your face. I make no apologies for the sex which appears in my books aimed at adults. I even include mild sexuality in my adolescence series that I have been doing, because to deny sex is to deny reality. It is as much a part of life as having to use the bathroom. In fact, it is, in my opinion, the best recreational activity ever devised. However, on occasion, I like to make light of it as a way make a hopefully profound statement about something.

THE WHOLE STORY

Daddy's car roared past Franklin into the woods.
. Curious, he followed the car
and saw Daddy and Aunt Jane
in a passionate embrace.

Little Franklin found this so exciting

LOVE: FROM THE DARKNESS TO THE LIGHT

that he could hardly contain himself,
as he ran to his nearby home
and started to tell his mother.

"Mummy, I was at the playground
and I saw Daddy's car go
into the woods with Aunt Jane,
and what I saw. What I saw."

"I went back to look
and he was giving Aunt Jane
a big kiss, and then
he helped her take off her shirt."

"Then Aunt Jane helped
Daddy take his pants off.
Then Aunt Jane., oh my mummy,
what she did to daddy."

At this point Mummy cut him off and said,
"Franklin, this is such an interesting story,
let's save the rest of it for supper time.
I want to see Daddy's reaction."

At the dinner table that evening,
Mummy asked little Franklin to tell his story.
So he did so with great glee,
Thinking all there would be pleased.

Franklin said, "I was at the playground
and I saw Daddy's car go into the woods with Aunt Jane.
I went back to look and he was giving Aunt Jane
a big kiss, then he helped her take off her shirt."

"Then Aunt Jane helped Daddy take his pants off.
Then Aunt Jane and Daddy started doing the same thing

LOVE: FROM THE DARKNESS TO THE LIGHT

that Mummy and Uncle Bill used to do
when Daddy was away on business.

Moral: Always listen to the whole story.

www.ingramcontent.com/pod-product-compliance
Lightning Source LLC
Chambersburg PA
CBHW061322040426
42444CB00011B/2734